Nourishing Body and Soul

Nourishing Body and Soul

101 Healthy Ways to Be Fit and Glorify God

III John 2.
"I pray that you may
enjoy good health in body
and soul".
                    NRP.

Norman R.
Piersma

Pleasant Word
A Division of WINEPRESS PUBLISHING

Printed in the United States of America

Packaged by Pleasant Word, a division of WinePress Publishing, PO Box 428, Enumclaw, WA 98022. The views expressed or implied in this work do not necessarily reflect those of Pleasant Word, a division of WinePress Publishing. Ultimate design, content, and editorial accuracy of this work are the responsibilities of the author.

All scripture references are taken from the Holy Bible, New Living Translation, copyright 1996. Used by permission of Tyndale House Publishers, Inc., Wheaton, Illinois 60189. All rights reserved.

ISBN 1-4141-0201-1
Library of Congress Catalog Card Number: 2004093461

Dedication

I dedicate this book:

To my wife Donna, and daughters Alicia, Anne and Patricia who backed me in prayer, encouraged me and joined me in the quest for wholeness.

To the Inter Varsity Christian Fellowship who reached me on the campus of the Michigan State University. They were instrumental in my spiritual maturity and, by way of the Urbana Missions Conference in 1951, was key to my being open to a missionary call, training and appointment.

To the Latin America Mission who recruited us in the person of Dr. R. Kenneth Strachan. The LAM trained us in Costa Rica and assigned us to work in Colombia. There we planted churches, directed animal projects in community development and founded Christian Care for Colombian Children. May the Lord be pleased to use the LAM in finishing the task in the Latin World.

My wife, three daughters, and oldest grandchild as they were in 1992. Left to right: Patricia Joy our youngest, Donna my wife, Anne Elizabeth our middle daughter, Jessica Jane (the daughter of Alicia Jane), and of Alicia Jane our oldest.

Contents

Foreword

What a privilege to write this foreword! My husband and I became acquainted with the author and his lovely wife about the time he was diagnosed with metastatic melanoma cancer. We saw how they immediately sprang into action taking charge of Dr. Piersma's health. It was amazing! I never witnessed such forward thinking in my life; their entire demeanor was positive and upbeat.

But even more than that, their faith in God was without waver. They trusted Him, they believed what the Word of God said—it was truth, it was right, they demonstrated total faith. Their commitment to the approach he writes about, both in their faith and taking the necessary steps to restore his body to health, was demonstrably evident at the outset and has continued through these long years.

To know someone who has defeated cancer is an awesome experience. It is to recognize that you can trust this person. He's lived through it! Norm, my wise friend, you are greatly valued for your conquest of what could have been an overpowering evil. Donna, my dear and loyal friend, you are every bit a part of this triumph. Together you did it, you are doing it, you are a powerful and persuasive couple in your stand for principles of health and total well being—physical and spiritual.

The reader who takes these things to heart will benefit greatly—their lives will be enriched in immeasurable ways.

Helen Kooiman Hosier
April 2004

Acknowledgements

I am grateful to:

The Aurora Foundation who has faithfully carried out the mission of the late Anthony Rossi in offering career-foreign missionaries a retirement home in the Bradenton Missionary Village.

My fellow members of the Village Writers Club who critiqued and encouraged. Special thanks to the scrutiny of writers Gloria Altenbernt and Betty Johnson.

The volunteer staff of the Village Computer Club who came to my aid instantly. They are Hardy Hayes, Leverne Wenner and Gerald Dallimore.

My golfing buddies Allen Wilson, John Tieszen and Charles Nielsen. They afforded me the breaks I needed to relax.

Our home church. Immanuel Church of Holland MI which catechized and discipled us, commissioned us, sent us out to the foreign mission field and partnered with us for forty years.

Wade Barwick who welcomed us to The Tabernacle several years ago and continues to do so each week as we bless one another in wellness.

Jack Watts who on the very day he married our widowed daughter Alicia, told me to write a book. And with the skill of a publisher, which he is, took out his pen and outlined the very format I used.

The Village Men's Prayer Meeting headed by Hudson Shedd, Fred Boldt and Ken Solomon. We meet four mornings a week at 7:30 A.M. and "bring to the Lord's attention" village needs, area requests, national crises and goings-on all over the world. That clears the deck for good writing!

John Buck, my fellow villager, who holds me accountable and truly prays me through whatever God directs me to do.

Helen K. Hosier, author and writer of over sixty books, who whispered to me via e-mail, *Norman, you can do it!*

My wife, Donna Mae, has been with me all the way. She did all of the final proof reading.

Jesus my Lord and Savior. He made me whole—He keeps me well. He'll take me home. All glory goes to Him!

Introduction

The purpose of this book is *education*. If one doesn't change, education has not happened. New information is interesting but it must effect a change to be meaningful.

In these documents I do not mean to sound definitive. Apart from God's Word, there is very little on earth that is a final answer. We'll finally see things totally true only when we are in heaven. It's then that we'll know it all. Isn't that what 1 Corinthians 13:12 is saying?

"Now we see things imperfectly as in a poor mirror, but then we will see everything with perfect clarity. All that I know now is partial and incomplete, but then I will know everything completely, just as God knows me now."

Other than the basic truth given us by divine revelation, we can not be dogmatic about most things. "What about science?", you may ask. George Santayana gave the best definition I've ever seen. "Science is neither a method nor a body of knowledge. It is a body of changing, learned opinion aspiring to be true. There are certain facts about nature and history. Our grasp of these facts is constantly changing."

In this book I have dozens of bits and pieces of information that I feel are valuable today. Even though new insights will appear tomorrow, you can benefit by incorporating certain elements for personal experimentation.

The reader will eventually go to the appendix and find out how one can research certain observations more profoundly.

My goal is to get you to see what wellness is all about. And to appreciate that body, mind and soul have an innate propensity to heal itself. Wellness depends on how fully we cooperate with our multi-trillions of cells, facilitating them with all they need to work and reproduce.

Even though I studied medicine five years, I experienced a giant paradigm shift as I grew in practical and biblical knowledge. This book will challenge your opinions about healthcare and hopefully push your paradigm toward wholeness.

Prevention Beats Treatment

And the Lord said to Moses, "Place Aaron's staff permanently before the Ark of the Covenant as a warning to rebels. This should put an end to their complaints against me and prevent any further deaths."

—Numbers 17:10,11

If we only knew how many times the Lord's intervention has prevented our deaths. The big one He has prevented is our passing from this life to *eternal* death. By staying on the narrow road we can avoid the broad road that ends in hell (Matthew 7:14).

There is some *rebel* in all of us. We must choose carefully when to use our rebellious instincts. Or we could turn out to be another status quo conformist. Suppose we could *prevent* most of the illnesses that cause the premature deaths of 80 percent of Americans. Cases such as heart disease, diabetes, and cancer can be prevented.

Conventional medicine offers us the "preventive services" that help detect disease earlier. Even Medicare will pay for the colorectal screening, pap smears, mamograms and prostate screening.

But what has been prevented? Nothing. So what *is* the ounce of prevention that is better than a pound of cure?

Kenneth Cooper M.D. who coined the term *aerobics* and led the exercise craze in the 70s, helped us to understand that an exercise program is one of three major ingredients to avoiding devastating illnesses. The second is a healthy diet. Seven servings a day of fruits and vegetables is a must.

The third element needed to prevent killer diseases and insure optimal health is Nutritional Supplements. To make sure they are quality supplements is not easy. If you only look for the cheapest, you won't get quality.

Action Step *Praise your Redeemer. Don't wait until you are sick to start a program of prevention. Consider this as a warning to begin today and become pro-active. Choose to live well.*

Talk About Eye Openers

"I don't know whether he is a sinner," the man replied. "But I know this: I was blind, and now I see."

—John 9:25

Jesus was, no doubt, the world's greatest eye opener. He still is.

I've had two major eye opening experiences in my life. The first one came on Easter Day 1946 while serving in the U.S. Army Air Force. I became a Christian. Right there in that Army chapel I turned my life over to Jesus. I couldn't believe I had been blind to so many things before.

The second eye opener happened in Mexico forty-five years later where I went for the Gerson Therapy. One month before I had been given only six months to live due to metastatic melanoma cancer.

Donna and I arrived at the Gerson Clinic May 7, 1991. Within minutes I was given a huge glass of organic carrot juice. In fact, I was served six carrot and six green drinks each day. Meals were strictly vegetarian—little salt, tons of garlic, lots of flax seed oil, huge salads and baked potato every day.

There were patients from all the continents with every disease imaginable. Many of them were classified as "terminal" like I was.

But what was I *seeing?* Almost without exception, they were getting well. Even my tumors soon started to disappear.

The lectures helped us to understand what was happening. Two things, we were told, are the bottom-line causes of all diseases: a toxic condition and an inefficient immune system. The famous Dr. Max Gerson, a German Jew, devised a way to detoxify the body and boost the immune system. Now here is the eye opener—once the body's waste removal system functions well and the immune system is up to par . . . *the body heals itself of whatever.*

Action Step *Lord, open my eyes. There are answers. But many of them will not be found in the U.S.A. Keep your eyes peeled for new glimpses of truth because what you don't know can kill you.*

Will Doctors Change?

Jesus answered them, "Healthy people don't need a doctor—sick people do. I have come to call sinners to turn from their sins, not to spend my time with them who think they are already good enough."

—Luke 5:31

Healthy people . . . sick people. This was a popular proverb of that day which Jesus applied to the healing of the souls of sinners. In ancient China the role of the doctor was to keep the people well. If someone got sick, he stopped paying the doctor. Every household contributed to the physician's salary as long as everyone was well.

Monthly contributions stopped, however, when one of the family became ill. The health practitioner did all in his power to restore the sick person so he could once again count on a payment.

Can you imagine how such a system would impact healthcare in the U.S. today? There would be no money to be made in treating disease, only in preventing it. Doctors would be concerned about coaching assigned families in better choices of diet and lifestyle. Pharmaceutical companies would go bankrupt. We would soon become the healthiest people in the world. As it is now, the U.S. is 82nd in the effective prevention of disease among the 100 industrialized nations of the world.

Thomas Edison, our brilliant scientist and inventor, made this observation: "The doctor of the future will give no medicine, but will interest his patients in the care of the human frame, in diet and in the cause and prevention of disease . . . The physician of tomorrow will be the nutritionist of today."

That "tomorrow" is still in the future. But the "nutritionist," usually in the form of a Naturopath, is among us now. We could call on him before we become ill. The Chinese had it right—"an ounce of prevention is worth a pound of cure."

Action Step *Exalt His holy Name. Be convinced that wellness can be achieved and maintained. Find out where you can take the course "Get Healthy, Stay Balanced."*

Say No to Drugs

Her nights will be dark without a single lamp. There will be no happy voices of brides and grooms. This will happen because her merchants, who were the greatest in the world, deceived the nations with her sorceries.
—Revelation 18:23

The Greek word that is translated "sorceries" is *pharma-kia*. This word, as you can see, today, means *drugs*. The drug companies make pharmaceuticals for the pharmacies. This prophetic picture written 1900 years ago, is happening *now*, right under our noses. The greatest deception of the end times could very well be the universal acceptance of DRUGS.

Drugs have become such a pervasive influence in our society that most Americans take drugs every day, and do not even realize they are addicted. The recreational drugs are illegal and not socially accepted, with the acception of alcohol. The over-the-counter and prescription drugs are generally called "good" drugs.

Whether we are talking about illegal hard-core drugs, alcohol, colas or pharmaceuticals, some of the most underhanded methods ever seen are used to get people on drugs. Drugs are big business.

Their ads are very *deceptive*. The obvious results are devastating.

Our jails are filled with drug offenders. Our hospitals are obligated to treat the intoxicated abusers. And our funeral homes process the corpses of one hundred thousand patients a year that die of prescription *drugs*.

Drugs are the world's way of treating a symptom, be it a pain, unhappiness or a dare. The solution is looking at it God's way—living food and living water that lead to health and contentment. Drugs are always toxic. Drugs cannot heal anything.

Action Step *Start cleaning your medicine cabinet of all remedies that are drug based. Replace them with a few natural products that are made from nature's plants.*

Chronic Disorders Are Debilitating

And there was a woman in the crowd who had had a hemorrhage for twelve years. She had suffered a great deal from many doctors through the years and had spent everything she had to pay them, but she had gotten no better. In fact, she was worse.

—Mark 5:25–26

Is the general medical doctor of today better than they were two thousand years ago when treating a chronic condition? Andrew Weil M.D. was frank to admit that only 20 percent of the sick people have conditions for which conventional allopathic medicine is appropriate. He says that the doctors use drugs for everything and it doesn't work for the majority of problems.

A recent study at the John Hopkins University concluded that chronic diseases are not prevented by vaccines or cured by medicines. The major chronic disease killers—heart, cancer, stroke and diabetes are an extension of what people do or not do, as they go about the business of everyday living.

This is true. It's what we do or not do everyday that gets us in trouble. The lady with the chronic hemorrhage had a once-in-a-millennium chance to reach out and touch a physical Jesus for healing. You and I may not have this chance—we'd better have a game plan that reverses our chronic conditions. Or prevent them!

Whatever we do or don't do must be based on the fact that the body is *self-healing*. Our bodies have been programed to stay well.

All they need is our cooperation. Once we supply our cells with the air, exercise, water and nutrition they need, symptoms will never surface. The typical tell-tail signs of headache, cold hands, insomnia, fever and stomachache are warnings that a chronic killer is taking hold. Don't think you are a victim of bad luck—realize instead that there is something **you** can do.

Action Step *Begin to read extensively the books that explain clearly what you need to know to get healthy and stay healthy. See the book listing at the back of the book.*

Is Wearing Eye Glasses Inevitable?

Moses was 120 years old when he died, yet his eyesight was clear.
—Deuteronomy 34:7

NO was the answer of an attorney who wrote to the editor of *Health Freedom News*. In law school, at age twenty-five, he was fitted with glasses. A few years later he read that many years ago a Chinese emperor developed a system of eye exercises that would correct eye ailments and improve one's vision.

He, too, developed a system of eye exercises and within six months, he wrote, "I put my faith in the Lord and threw away my glasses." He wrote this testimonial forty years later when he still had 20/20 vision and no glasses. These are the exercises he does every other day:

Without moving your head, move your eyes from right to left and left to right, fifty times. Next make a large "X" fifty times. Then do the alphabet as if you were skywriting, one time. Next do a large figure 8 fifty times followed by an 8 on its side, fifty times. Do this every other day for two weeks and then double everything except the alphabet.

"Caution," writes the now retired lawyer, "don't do these exercises in church. The preacher kept looking at me. When he was making a point, I was moving my eyes from side to side as if to say no. Then later up and down as if to say yes. I think I ruined his sermon."

One more thing that is helpful is massaging the eyes. With your left center finger, massage your left eye and with your right center finger massage your right eye—several times a day. Granted, Moses didn't have so much fine print to read as we do. But let's go for it—keen eyesight right into our golden years. And without glasses!

Action Step *Lift up your eyes and praise Him. Prayerfully and faithfully exercise your precious eyes. Avoid ocular crutches as long as you can.*

Guard Your Heart

Above all else, guard your heart, for it affects everything you do.
—Proverbs 4:23

This good advice was written 2,900 years ago. But it covers even more territory today. Then the author was speaking only figuratively. He pleads with us to keep the center of our being pure since it dictates our every thought, word and deed.

Now look at today's verse from a physical point of view. Why do we need to guard carefully our primary organ, the heart? It not only affects everything we do, its failure is our leading cause of death. The American Heart Association reports that one of us has a heart attack every twenty seconds and every minute another dies of it.

What a tragedy to learn that there would be no such thing as heart attacks if blood were allowed to flow freely through the coronary arteries. One way to guard our hearts and keep the blood easily flowing is to give green salads a high priority. As far back as 1961 the AMA declared in their Journal that 90 to 97 percent of heart disease could be prevented with a vegetarian diet.

Another important way to guard our heart would be eat heart healthy *fats*. "There are fats that kill," says Udo Erasmus, Ph.D ."and fats that heal." The principle oil that heals the heart is Omega 3. It is an essential fatty acid that we must have in our diet. Here are several reasons why :

Omega 3 makes our platelets less sticky.
This fatty acid makes our red blood cells more flexible.
Omega 3 lowers our blood pressure.
This amazing oil stabilizes the heart beat.
Omega 3 lowers the triglyceride factor.

> **Action Step** *Love God with all your heart. Add UDO's Choice oil supplement to your daily regimen to get all the Omegas one needs. Avoid the animal fats that kill.*

Did God Prescribe Food?

And God said, "Look, I have given you the seed-bearing plants throughout the earth and all the fruit trees for your food."

—Genesis 1:29

The picture here is God giving Adam and Eve an orientation on how to live and what to do. The scene takes place in the Garden of Eden where they are surrounded by the plants and trees God is talking about. They and their progeny did very well on this vegetarian diet. So well that they lived for hundreds of years.

For ten generations mankind lived an average of 912 years. Right after the great flood God gave permission to eat some "clean" animals since the flood had destroyed all vegetation. The people evidently enjoyed eating flesh but it took its toll. Within ten generations the lifespan had dropped down to one hundred years at the end of Genesis.

In 1991 I was told by my oncologist that I was "terminal" due to metastatic melanoma cancer. Basically, it was the same diet of raw fruits and vegetables—which God gave to Adam and Eve—that saved my life and restored my health. And it has been this same diet that has kept me in excellent health ever since.

Raw fruits, vegetables, grains and nuts are called *living food*. Living because the enzymes and phytochemicals are alive. Cooked and processed foods are classified as *dead food*. When God created man He designed him to consume raw plant food. Our bodies are living organisms, made of living cells which require living food.

Where do we get all this good, live food? We have three basic sources. We grow as much we can in our own organic vegetable garden. Secondly, we praise God for an organic produce farm that has a stand for the public each weekend. And we visit the local health store that sells a great selection of fresh greens and veggies.

Action Step *Clap your hands for joy. Start leaving out dead foods from your diet one at a time. You'll soon be on the stuff God prescribed.*

Save Your Hearing

A deaf man with a speech impediment was brought to him . . . He put his fingers into the man's ears . . . And looking up to heaven, he sighed and commanded, "Be open." Instantly the man could hear perfectly and speak plainly.

—Mark 7:32–36

As much as we would like to pray, "Be open," as we minister to our deaf and hard-of-hearing friends, more than likely, we'll not see instant healing. Hearing restoration is very difficult. What we do know is that all of us will experience hearing loss during our life time.

To prevent excessive hearing loss we must practice hearing conservation. The object is to protect the tiny hair cells inside the cochlea of the inner ear. Loud and prolong noise can permanently destroy these hair cells, causing hearing loss. The damage may be gradual, painless and invisible, but it's permanent and very real.

We start life with a fixed number of hair cells. As we age, they begin to die off naturally. And as we expose ourselves to excess noise, more cells are destroyed. Fortunately, hearing loss caused by noise can be prevented. It is advised to always wear hearing protectors when you are exposed to hazardous noise.

Likewise, the natural hair cell depletion can be cut down some by the very same means that we use to stay well and balanced. Anything that gives optimal health will protect your hearing also.

The nutritional supplement that's beneficial in all hearing conditions is the herb *Ginkgo biloba*. Take eighty mgs a day as a precaution.

Action Step *Listen to His voice. The hair cells you have are the only ones you'll ever get. Think up ways to reduce the noise in your life. Seek peace and quiet.*

We Need to Hear This

Be on guard. Stand true to what you believe. Be courageous. Be strong. And everything you do must be done in love.

—1 Corinthians 16:13–14

Here we note five charges in this exhortation—all in the present tense. That is, this is the way believers are to live. These things are to be constantly carried out.

Could it be that the hardest of the five is to *stand true to what you believe?* Because much of what we believe has to constantly be revised and updated as we grow in the knowledge of the Word.

Four hundred years ago the famous Francis Bacon said this: "Man prefers to believe what he prefers to be true."

Other than the unchanging absolutes of the Gospel, our ideas are in constant flux. New and "proven" information help us define more clearly what we believe. What do you think about the core belief expressed by Dr. David Frahm?

"We are to be responsible stewards to our own health." He then gives these reasons: "I believe God can directly intervene in our health to accomplish His sovereign purposes, but health is primarily a reflection of God's universal law of cause and effect. A man reaps what he sows. How we feed and care for our bodies does impact our health, the health of our offspring and the effectiveness of our service to God."

Do these statements affect what you *prefer to believe?* Let's remember that the word *believe* is composed of two words, *be* and the old Dutch word *lief* meaning *love*. To believe something is to be in love with the idea of such.

Even though I spent five years at Michigan State University studying nothing but medicine, I was taught very little about what it means to be well. At age sixty-four I had to form a whole new paradigm.

I had to lovingly form a new model in which I could believe.

Action Step *Be strong! Do not forget that being on guard and being courageous only works when it is wrapped in love.*

Live a Long and Healthy life

I will satisfy them with a long life and give them my salvation.

—Psalm 91:16

I believe that "a long life" is part of the salvation package. Anyone who complies with the Bible's guidelines will have the 120 years potential as promised in Genesis 6:3. This longevity need not be hampered with disease and feebleness.

It is predicted that by the year 2040 as many as one million people will celebrate their 100th birthday. But few people would want to reach such a milestone if they knew they wouldn't have the strength to cut the cake.

God's gift of long life is not just extending life but is concerned with increasing our vital, disease-free years. Harvard Medical School conducted a study of 159 people who lived to 100. They identified factors that may have contributed to their long life.

Flossing teeth decreases bacteria that are implicated in heart disease. **Supplementing** with vitamin E, selenium and alpha lipoic acid is a positive practice along with taking flax seed oil for the beneficial Omega 3 fatty acid. **Work and exercise** were found in their lives in the form of stretching, weight lifting and aerobics.

Eating right usually meant making the salad the biggest part of dinner. Raw fruits and vegetables are high in phyto-chemicals, minerals and anti-oxidants.

I doubt if Harvard included questions in their study about spiritual beliefs. Wholeness in Jesus can be a big factor in staying well. I got serious about these longevity factors late in life. My prospects of living long are not good but these last years are proving to be free of all the problems old age are "supposed" to bring.

Action Step *Thank God for your salvation. Don't follow the example of Israelites who died prematurely in the desert for disobedience as described in Psalm 90. Rather be like Moses who died at 120 and "was strong as ever."*

Living Water: Human Body

If you only knew the gift God has for you and who I am, you would ask me, and I would give you living water.

—John 4:10

With two thirds of the earth covered with water, it becomes so mundane. Realizing, however, that we are 78% water at birth and about 50% at death, we can better appreciate the analogy Jesus makes. Next to oxygen, water is the most vital agent to sustain life.

There can neither be life on earth nor life eternal without the living water of Jesus.

In May of 1998 we stood ankle-deep in the Jordan river and "baptized" ourselves by tossing handfuls of *maim chaim,* Jordan's living water, on our heads—vowing to think His thoughts, on our hearts—**vowing** a pure devotion, on our hands—vowing to dedicate our work and on our feet—vowing to walk worthy of his calling. From there we went to an oasis called En Gedi where we drank from a spring of clear, cold, living water.

Because water gives life, physically and spiritually, we must choose our water sources carefully. The prophet Jeremiah warns us in 2:13 about the dangers of drinking old cistern water. Today's hydrologists warn us about drinking tap water. We may have to buy pure drinking water. One of the best is made by reverse osmosis. A system can be installed in your kitchen.

Here is a way to calculate your daily water intake requirement: Take the number of pounds your body weighs and divide that number in half. The result is the number of fluid ounces of water you should drink each day. A two hundred pound man is looking at 100 fluid ounces or about twelve 8 ounce cups. WATER, that is, not sodas or coffee.

Action Step *O God, my soul thirsts for You! Measure out, each day, in a large pitcher, the amount you should drink. Make sure your drinking water is free of clorine, antibiotics, heavy metals, disinfectant byproducts and bacteria. It is important that you drink pure water.*

Plan to Give Birth Naturally

Then Pharaoh, the king of Egypt, gave this order to the Hebrew midwives Shiphrah and Puah: "When you help the Hebrew women give birth, kill all the boys as soon as they are born. Allow only the girl babies to live." ". . . the Hebrew women are very strong. They have their babies so quickly that we can not get there in time."

—Exodus 1:15–16,19

Birth is a natural process. Women have always helped each other go through this God-honoring experience. The life-saving techniques of child birthing is passed on from one generation to another. Only until recently it's been the midwives that delivered most of the babies. In The King James and the New International Version keep the reference to "the delivery stool" in Pharaoh's command.

Today they are refered to as "birthing chairs." These sturdy stools look like a padded toilet seat. Seated on this stool, the laboring mother is greatly helped by gravity. She is also in a much better position to PUSH. The midwife has to get down on the floor to receive the newborn by guiding its head and turning it for the final exit.

Conventional medicine, it seems, has categorized birth as a disease by insisting that it take place, not at home, but in a hospital.

They do not use the birthing stool. It's too inconvenient for the doctors. They prefer the supine, spread-eagle position. This probably causes so many *distocia* cases that call for a C-section. About 25 percent of births in this country are carried out by C-section. Where midwives are in charge, only 3 percent need this emergency operation. From the beginning of time natural practitioners have known that squatting is the proper position for giving birth.

Holland has the best birth survival rate with 80 percent born at home.

We rank twenty-first in the world and have only 20 percent born at home.

Action Step *Praise His holy name for natural and spiritual birth. Get in touch with the Seventh Day Adventists who have the best track record using midwives. Be brave.*

Oxygen's Other Side

And the Lord God formed a man's body from the dust of the ground and breathed into it the breath of life. And man became a living person.

—Genesis 2:7

Since the time God breathed life into Adam, air that is, *oxygen* has been a primary sustainer of biological life. We can live five weeks without food, five days without water but only five minutes without oxygen. It is a precious gift of God but it can turn on us.

Oxygen becomes our enemy by turning into a *free radical.* The radicals act like insane terrorists damaging vital tissues. This eventually results in heart disease, cancer or one of another 100 degenerative conditions.

At the same time God breathed life into Adam, He programed the body to fight and subdue the ever-present free radicals. To do this *antioxidants* are produced. Anyone in top physical condition should have sufficient antioxidants to keep the enemy in check—up to a certain point.

Almost any area of today's lifestyle sparks some free radical production. Stress, excessive exercise, air pollution, drinks other than water and many of our favorite foods produce significant numbers of free radicals. The answer is twofold. We must practice a more temperate lifestyle and take the right supplements.

We should take 1,000 milligrams of vitamin C, a buffered ascorbate, twice a day. Each day we should take 400 mg of natural E, 100 mg of alpha lipoic acid, 100 mg of grape seed extract and 50 to a 100 mg of coenzyme Q-10, preferable in a softgel of coconut oil. This could add up to a wellness investment of less than two dollars a day.

Action Step *With all your breath, praise Him. Prayerfully pace yourself. Cut down stress. Add broccoli, cauliflower, carrots, tomatoes, nuts, onions, and garlic to your menu. Get quality supplements—cheap ones don't work. In about three months you'll experience the impact.*

Posture Is Important

It is like a person who builds a house on a strong foundation laid upon the underlying rock. When the flood waters rise and break against the house, it stands firm because it is well built.

—Luke 6:48

We spend so much time slouched in front of a computer, TV and in meetings that we need to know about the importance of posture. It's a *well built* temple/ body that is going to stand *firm* and erect. This is only possible when our muscles are strong enough to hold everything in place.

People in the day of Jesus didn't have to worry much about posture because their active lifestyle kept every muscle in good shape. To be as fit as they were, our program needs to include flexibility exercises and weight training. It's the usual stretches that produce flexibility.

Both weight bearing and weight lifting are necessary. Weight bearing exercises for good aerobics are stair-stepping, running and walking. They prevent osteoporosis and build up your heart and lungs. This helps you avoid being one of the 50 percent of the population who are dying of heart and circulation disease.

Weight lifting is very necessary for all adults. Without it we will lose 2 percent a year of our muscle mass. For a better posture, focus on strengthening the muscles between the shoulders. Ladies can do this by sitting at the end of a bench with a five pound dumbbell in each hand at shoulder height. Press the dumbbells out and in, so they nearly touch above the head. Lower and repeat.

For the men, grasp a barbell with appropriate weights a bit broader than shoulder width and bring it up a little above the collar bone. Press the weight up until the arms are fully extended over the head. Pause, lower to starting position and repeat.

Action Step *Bow before Him. Work out with weights three days a week and on alternate days, do the aerobic training you prefer. Choose to build a house, your body/temple, to stand firm for good posture.*

Who Is Your Hero?

The angel of the Lord appeared to him and said, "Mighty hero, the Lord is with you." "Sir," Gideon replied, "if the Lord is with us, why has all this happened to us?"

—Judges 6:12–13

Gideon is one of my heroes. Carey Reams is another one. About the same time in 1945 that I began basic training in the Army Air Force, Major Carey Reams Ph.D. and father of three, was a part of General McArthur's troops recapturing the Philippine Islands. He was seriously wounded, lost one eye and wasn't expected to live. He underwent forty-one operations but sensed he was losing the battle.

Finally in December of 1950 he was given permission to be driven to a Kathryn Kuhlman healing meeting in Butler, PA. He was convinced that getting to a miracle service was his last hope. Miss Kuhlman called to him, "Stand up, come to the front and throw your crutches aside in Jesus' name." Carey struggled to get to his feet. He began to inch forward, dropped one crutch, and later another. By the time he got to the front he was totally healed.

In the ensuing years Dr. Reams became very successful as a chemical consultant to the largest food growers. At the same time he enjoyed raising his children in such a way that they were never ill. This caught the attention of his neighbors and fellow church members. He was swamped with requests for advice on how to get well and stay well. Through prayer and fasting the Lord gave Reams a testing tool he later called Reams Biological Theory of Ionization. His premise was that most disease is the result of a mineral deficiency.

He was fiercely persecuted by the FDA and proudly admitted he was jailed more often than the apostle Paul. He was imprisoned for advising the parents of a two-year-old with terminal leukemia to give the girl a cleansing fast of distilled water and fruit juice. Later, his Wellness Camp in Florida was closed and he was put in prison.

Action Step *Give Him all the glory. Pray for the individuals and organizations that are fighting for health freedom.*

Running Can Change You

The Lord gave special strength to Elijah. He tucked his cloak into his belt and ran ahead of Ahab's chariot all the way to the entrance of Jezreel.

—1 Kings 18:46

The distance between Mt. Carmel and Jezreel was over twenty miles. Unless Elijah was a well trained runner he could not have done this—the miraculous was involved here. It may take a miracle to get you going, off the couch and on to the track. You've tried before to change things. First it was diet, then vitamins and exercises. Maybe it will take running for you to experience some positive, permanent changes.

The first thing you should do is determine to start running. It's a leap of faith because it'll take unwavering determination the first weeks. Getting back in shape is one day at a time. The painful moments that accompany your first attempts at running are quickly replaced by a sense of accomplishment.

Actually we are designed to run. We are built to be long distance runners. Slow runners, but long distance as we get used to it. The first week we should only walk. The second week try running for thirty seconds for every five minutes of walking. The third week break into a run for a full minute every five minutes. By the sixth week you should be walking and running equal amounts of time. By the twelfth week your intervals should be running for five minutes and walking for one minute.

You need a pair of running shoes. A mid-priced stability shoe is a good choice. Size is meaningless. You need a thumb's width between the end of your longest toe and the end of the shoe. Author John Bingham, in his *Beginner's Guide to the Joy of Running* declares that we humans are really a "running machine."

Action Step *Worship the Lord as you run. You don't have to run fast to be a real runner because there is no need for speed. The Lord gave Elijah special strength to run and do what he was supposed to do. He can do it for you also.*

Why Are You Sick So Often?

Don't drink only water. You ought to drink a little wine for the sake of your stomach, because you are sick so often.

—1 Timothy 5:23

The most important thing you can do to help restore the natural elimination process is address the real cause, *poor digestion*. The apostle Paul knew, instinctively, that Timothy's being sick so often came from the root cause of poor digestion.

Why is a *little* red wine so good for you? First of all it helps digestion by stimulating the production of stomach acid without injuring the mucosal lining. Also, studies show that the subjects that drink two small glasses of red wine each day had 30 percent to 50 percent less risk of heart disease and stroke. It's the resveratrol in grape skins that increases HDL (good) cholesterol and is an antioxidant.

Proper digestion requires two things—enough hydrochloric acid HCl and enough production of *digestive enzymes*. One of three Americans have low HCl production. Most golden agers should supplement. Low HCl results in partial digestion. This brings on more parasites and an overgrowth of unwanted bacteria. Poor diet, aging and chronic use of medication/antibiotics contribute to the stomach's inability to produce enough acid.

Antacids make the problem worse. They neutralize the little HCl you are producing. They spell temporary relief but the problem will get worse. What is needed is a supplement that includes both the HCl and a full range of digestive enzymes. It is called a "full spectrum enzyme formula." The multi-enzyme tablet should also have Betaine HCl, Pepsin, Bromelain, Ox Bile Extract, Cellulase as well as all the basic three constituents of pancreatin: Protease, Amylase and Lipase.

***

Action Step *Thank God you needn't be sick. By eating more vegetables and by taking two full spectrum tablets after a large meal and one tablet after breakfast and lunch, you can prevent heart burn, hiatal hernia and indigestion. And don't forget that a little grape wine may also help.*

Sunlight Actually Prevents Cancer

For God made two great lights, the sun and the moon to shine upon the earth.
—Genesis 1:16

God made them and they were good. So good that without them there would be no life on planet earth. The key to all life is photosynthesis. It gives us the world of plants. We and all of the animal kingdom get our nutrition, energy and vitality by consuming plants of all kinds.

Many people believe that exposure to the sun causes cancer. The latest studies, however, deny this. In the prominent journal *Cancer* Dr. William Grant reports that in 506 regions of the country they found a close inverse correlation between cancer mortality and levels of ultraviolet B light. In other words, the more sun exposure there is, the less cancer is found. The strongest inverse correlation is with breast, colon and ovarian malignancies.

Does this mean that excessive sun exposure does *not* contribute to skin cancer? No, it can cause it. However, the basic cause of skin cancer is an imbalance of omega fats in one's diet. Having an excess of omega 6 and a deficiency of omega 3, puts people at a higher risk of developing skin cancer when exposed to excess sun.

If you avoid the sun and don't change your diet, you will lower your risk of skin cancer. But, at the same time, you'll increase your risk of far more common and deadlier cancers. It behooves us to both get a daily dose of sun *and* make sure we balance our omega intake.

The sun gives us a cancer defense in the form of vitamin D. It's the sun's ultraviolet B that prompts the body to synthesize this important vitamin. It also has the role of maintaining normal blood levels of calcium and phosphorus, assuring us of good bone health.

By the way, people who soak up a little sunlight every day are less likely to feel fatigued.

Action Step *Thank God every day for the sun. Add to your daily diet one tablespoon of flax seed oil for extra omega 3.*

Let's Wash Our Hands More Often

They noticed that some of Jesus' disciples failed to follow the usual Jewish ritual of hand washing before eating.

—Mark 7:2

Instructions for personal hygiene were given to the Israelites soon after escaping the slavery of Egypt. Washing their hands became a life-long habit as well as a religious observance. The custom of keeping their hands clean along with burying their body wastes, aided the Jews to survive in the midst of worldwide epidemics.

Only in the last one hundred years have we known how wise it is to wash our hands frequently. What happens is that when we touch our eyes, nose and mouth, we innoculate these sensitive tissues with scores of bad germs. Our fingertips pick up, constantly, infectious organisms that quickly penetrate our facial openings.

We now know that up to 80 percent of all our illnesses in a lifetime will enter the body through the ocular and nasal membranes. What ever we get on our fingertips is auto-innoculated into the eyes, nose and mouth. With new antibiotic resistant germs, hygiene is more important than ever.

Any hand soap will work. But there are special formulas in the health store that do the job better. The object is to relieve our over-worked immune systems. Each disease producing bacteria that starts multiplying in our eyes and nasal passages, requires a battle to eliminate the intruder.

One way to monitor your immune system's activity is to watch, in your blood chemistry reports, your albumin level. The lower the number, the higher is the intensity of activity. The closer you can get it to the optimum of 5, the better you will feel and the longer you will live. Your number will rise the more you wash your hands.

Action Step *Raise your hands to honor Him. God has told us to wash our hands, so do it routinely. Scrub, especially, your fingertips and under the nails. Wash four to ten times a day the rest of your life. Give your immune system a break.*

Are You Looking for a Cure?

At that very time, he cured many people of their various diseases,
and cast out evil spirits and restored sight to the blind.

—Luke 7:21

Even today the Roman Catholic priests in Spanish-speaking countries are called *Curas*. This comes from the word *curar* meaning to cure. For hundreds of years the only ones who had the herbs and the knowledge to use them, were the monks. Ill people found a "cure" by seeking the remedies of the priests.

Now we live in a day when there are so many "incurable" diseases. We watch our elderly relatives suffer from these horrible infirmities. We live in fear, as victims, wondering when a killer bug will strike us or when the inevitable cancer will appear.

Each year billions of dollars are budgeted for medical research to find cures. Cynthia Foster M.D. says, "There is no cure for anything." She goes on to explain that medicines do not cure. Doctors do not cure. Surgery and drugs do not cure. The only two agents that do cure are God and our cells.

The cells of our tissues and organs bring about healing and a cure by replacing themselves with stronger and more vigorous cells.

The body is always in the process of healing itself. It does this, however, only when we assist the body in it's cleansing modes and supplying the best of nutrients. Add to this an abundance of pure water. There are no incurable diseases, only incurable people.

People, that is, who are not willing to change in order to get well.

There are ways that people can take control of their lives. By taking responsibility, they can bring themselves back to health again. Our bodies needn't be constantly in an emergency cure mode. There is a way to prevent most of the serious killers. By following natural healing programs, we can maintain our temples.

Action Step *Look to Him for a true cure. No matter if the doctor says there is no cure for it, the body can cure itself. So treat it right, give it love and laughter. Above all, prayerfully administer beneficial nutrients.*

21

How's Your Liver?

The king of Babylon now stands at the fork, uncertain whether to attack Jerusalem or Rabbah. He will call on his magicians to use divination. They will cast lots by shaking arrows from the quiver. They will inspect the livers from their animal sacrifices.

—Ezekiel 21:21

All important decisions in the ancient Near East were made with the help of divination, attempting to find the will of the gods. The only importance they gave the liver was in future telling. They had no idea what a key player the liver is in body detoxification.

David Frahm ND wrote that there is only one degenerative disease of the human body—*toxic overload*. Everything else is a symptom. How's your liver? is a good question because the state of this organ and how well it functions determines how well you are and how long you'll live.

Our livers, today, have to work overtime to remove from the blood thousands of chemicals, pollutants and medicines that contaminate us. The food we eat, the liquids we drink and the air we breathe saturate us with toxins. We have to prayerfully seek ways of dumping these toxic loads and fortify our over-challenged liver.

We can get rid of toxins everyday by deep breathing, drinking more pure water and by exercising to the point of sweating profusely. Furthermore, we can take Milk Thistle extract, one of the great herbs of all time. Take this natural supplement, 175 mg with each meal. It will assist the liver to more effectively keep our blood clean of all toxins.

As usual, diet plays an important role in liver maintenance. Eat a diet that has a large percentage of raw foods. Also, include fresh juices along with BarleyMax. Legumes detoxify excess ammonia.

Action Step *Thank the Lord for knowing what you can do each day to keep your temple/body more pure. Don't forget the four reasons for poor liver: toxins, improper diet, overeating and use of medicines and drugs.*

Can You Stand Alone?

But Daniel made up his mind not to defile himself by eating the food and wine given to them by the king.

—Daniel 1:8

Daniel and his family were carried off as captives to the wicked city of Babylon. There he was separated from the godly influence of his parents and family. He was put into a special boarding school that was humanistic and pagan.

He realized that he would have to adapt to this foreign culture by learning the language and understanding the new ways of doing things. But when it came to the basic issue of eating and drinking, he *made up his mind not to defile himself.*

He could have felt bitter toward God who permitted the enemy to conquer Jerusalem. Then to go one step further, by dragging him off to a foreign land. But, Daniel, instead of forgetting the moral standards of his parents, stood alone with his scriptural convictions.

John McDougall M.D. points out that today we all have the option to eat and drink like kings. The Standard American Diet is as rich or richer than that of the kings of old. Dr. McDougall says that we have the option to continue to *defile* ourselves or choose the more simple diet of fresh vegetables and water as Daniel requested.

Daniel was a winner over and over again. God gave him the courage and strength to stand alone. He knew where to draw the line. The world calls us to eat, drink and be merry. Even if it means standing alone, are you willing to opt for sustenance God would approve of?

Action Step *Praise the God of heaven with Daniel. He interpreted dreams and sat quietly with hungry lions, but it started with his determining the kind of diet that was best for him physically and what would bring glory to God. The majority rarely choose what's right. Jesus said that the road is narrow and only a few find it. Be prepared to stand alone.*

What is Nutrition?

Why spend your money on food that does not give you strength? Why pay for food that does you no good?

—Isaiah 55:2

It was about six hundred years before Christ that God asked these questions. The context tells us that this is a figure of speech with a spiritual application. But metaphors that are used are generally true. Therefore, the history of selling unhealthy food goes back many years. Why don't more of us ask these questions today?

For food to give us strength and do us good, it has to be nutritious. Webster tells us that nutrition is "the sum of the processes by which an animal or plant absorbs and utilizes food substances." Researcher Micheal Dye further defines *nutrition* saying that if it can be used by your body to build healthy, vibrant, new, living cells IT IS NUTRITION. If it cannot be used for the above, it is NOT nutrition.

Nutrients come most freely from LIVE food. That is, raw fruit and vegetables directly from the tree or plant. Once these have been steamed, cooked, baked or preserved, they have become DEAD food. Why? Because the protein and minerals have been changed and the enzymes totally killed.

We know that enzymes are the life force, the activating power that helps all other nutrients to work in the body. Living cells need nutrients from live foods. The Lord asks us why we spend our hard-earned money on so called *food* when it won't pass the test of producing strength. Only good food will do us good. Beware of the market that also has a pharmacy. What are they telling us?

Buy our food, eat our food, get sick, and now take our drugs?

Knowing that diet and lifestyle are the cause of almost all diseases, *nutrition* takes on a greater importance. Let's pay for real food.

Action Step *O Creator, we adore You. The next time you shop for food, spend more time in the produce section. Give living foods a higher priority.*

Holiness or Destruction

Or don't you know that your body is the temple of the Holy Spirit? God will bring ruin upon anyone who ruins this temple. For God's temple is holy, and you Christians are that temple.

—1 Corinthians 6:19a, 3:17

On the first Good Friday, two thousand years ago, God the Holy Spirit changed His address from the Holy of Holies in the man-made temple, to the hearts of believers. This gives Christians great dignity. At the same time it puts on us profound responsibility regarding the maintenance of our body/temples.

By God's Spirit residing in us, we are declared holy. We are expected to reflect this fact in every facet of life. This makes us accountable to God as to how we live, work, eat and sleep.

Today's verses warn us not to be careless. Because if we are, it could cause our ruin. The Lord evidently holds us responsible for getting sick. A holy temple and sickness do not go together. Jesus quoted Isaiah who said, "He took our sicknesses and removed our diseases" (Matthew 8:17).

By following the principles of Holy Scripture, we can carry out a lifestyle that prevents sickness and disease. Illness is not the will of God for His own people. However, we are still free to choose how we treat our temples. If we ignore the biblical ordinances, examples and commands, the ruin of our bodies is inevitable.

In fact, God will look the other way. This is God's way of bringing ruin on anyone who neglects his temple. In most cases, praying for healing will do no good. It's repentance and a new obedience that will restore health. Once we are forgiven, the Lord will guide us and give us the wisdom we need for total holiness.

Action Step *Holy, holy, holy, Lord God Almighty. Now that you know, be wise in working out a daily program of temple maitenance. Holiness is a lot more than saying your prayers. Seek a deeper understanding by reading the book,* Total Forgiveness.

Milk and Honey—Sounds Good

Be careful to obey. Then all will go well with you, and you will have many children in the land flowing with milk and honey, just as the Lord, the God of your ancestors, promised you.

—Deuteronomy 6:3

Sometimes the phrase "milk and honey" is used to describe the richness of the Promised Land. This was great for the Israelites to hear because in the wilderness they had very little of these delicious items. It turns out that most of what we translate into the English word *honey* was actually a syrup made of dates. The milk was usually goat milk, rarely drunk fresh but was soured into curds.

Our milk scenario today is so different. There is an unlimited supply for fresh milk and honey. David Frahm, Naturopath, routinely muscle tests all who seek his counsel. Neither milk nor honey get a passing grade. As a veterinarian I can attest to the fact that cow milk is for calves who need to grow from 100 lbs. to 300 lbs. in six months. It is very different from mother's milk that will help the baby double its weight in one year. Milk from cows is not a good food for humans. And the Bible warns us about honey—*Don't eat too much of it, or it will make you sick.*

There is one dairy product, however, that gets praise—*kefir.* Donna Gates in her book *Body Ecology Diet* says it is a nutritious, incredibly delicious food. The best kefir is made with fresh, raw goat milk. It is alkaline while cow milk is acidic. Simply add one and one half packets of starter, stir it, cover it and let it be on your counter top for twenty-four hours. Then refrigerate it to stop the fermentation process. Kefir assists in the digestion process, keeps the intestine free of parasites and is an excellent source of vitamin B12 which is essential for longevity.

> **Action Step** *I'm listening, Lord. Find a goat farm nearby and get fresh, unpasteurized milk. Order the starter culture packets by calling 1.800.511.2660. Eat kefir on an empty stomach alone or combine with blueberries, strawberries or cranberries. Enjoy!*

God's Will Is 120 Years

Then the Lord said, "My spirit will not put up with humans for such a long time, for they are only mortal flesh. In the future, they will live no more than 120 years."

—Genesis 6:3

At that time in history, God lowered man's longevity from many hundreds of years down to a maximum of 120. Roy Walford M.D., Ph.D. a leader in the field of aging, says that the 120 marker is scientifically correct to this day. It has been proven that you can extend your life, if you use the same mechanisms that gave rodents a 40 percent increase in life span.

These laboratory rodents were kept on a calorie-restricted diet and were compared to rodents that had free access to the same diet.

The restricted group were allowed to eat at certain times a predetermined amount of food. Whereas the free group could eat at any time and the amount they wanted. This do-as-you-please group didn't do very well compared to the long-living restricted group. A program for us who want to enjoy the full 120 years would require a lot of discipline.

The Hunza people of North Pakistan, to this day, enjoy a longevity whereby a substantial number of them live to be 120 years old. They are restricted in what they eat and how much they eat by the climate and steep terrain. They run out of food and have to fast a month each Spring. The body responds to this kind of rough regimen. It lasts much longer and stays very well.

What could we possibly do to live a longer, healthier life? First of all, we would have to eliminate all refined carbohydrates. Most breads and baked goods would have to go. Secondly, we would have to fill our stomachs primarily with, vegetables. Then we should always leave the table a little hungry. You can enjoy the sensation of a full stomach (it takes twenty minutes to realize you're full) while not incurring a high-calorie load.

Action Step *Live long here and eternally in Him. Restrict your calorie intake. This reduces the insulin level that slows aging.*

Choose Good Fun Food

Then he gave a gift to every man and woman in Israel: a loaf of bread, a cake of dates and a cake of raisins.

—2 Samuel 6:19

King David appreciated the way people accompanied him in bringing the Ark of God to the city of David. He showed his gratitude by giving each one a gift of food. This celebration called for a treat. Two of the sweetest foods in the Holy Land, even to this day, are raisins and dates. They translate into health.

Snacks are part of the American way of life. The first thing we are offered in our Sunday school class meeting is a refreshment of coffee and a snack. Too often the snacks we see in the stores could be classified as junk-foods (pseudo-foods). "Snacking is not the problem," says Dr. Frahm, "it is the kind of snacks."

David gave the Israelites a healthy snack. That's a good example to follow. Three thousand years ago and up until 1940, all food was organically grown. Today we must discriminate by choosing fresh, unprocessed and naturally grown snacks. Fresh and dried fruit can't be beat. Back in the thirties and forties my father kept a bushel of apples near the back door where we kids and our friends could help ourselves. Dad paid fifty cents a bushel.

Carrot and celery sticks provide an excellent source of vitamins and minerals. Raw nuts and seeds are another nutritious snack. Almonds seem to pack the most punch per cost unit. Among the hundreds of snack bars on the market today, there is one that stands head and shoulders above them all. It is the *Maple Nut Royale Bar.* It is made by Genesis Living Food Snacks.

Hallelujah Acres gives this bar a five star rating. It's ingredients are raw almonds, walnuts, pecans, macadamias, maple syrup and distilled water. This is a living food snack because it is totally raw.

The nuts have not been roasted and there are no additives, no chemicals. All the original enzymes are still there.

Action Step *Celebrate! Avoid the omnipresent vending machines. Choose living snacks. Follow David's example.*

What, No Breakfast?

But when you fast, comb your hair and wash your face. Then no one will suspect you are fasting, except your Father, who knows what you do in secret. And your Father, who knows all secrets, will reward you.

—Matthew 6:17–18

Jesus expected His followers to fast at regular intervals. When we are asked when we fast, I tell people that we fast everyday—all morning. People are shocked because they have been told that the most important meal of the day is breakfast.

There is evidence, however, to the contrary. Take the case of the Hunza people of West Pakistan. They are probably the healthiest people in the world. They eat only two meals a day, lunch and dinner. The men continue to work and participate in games well after the age of one hundred.

Some physiologists are suggesting our digestive systems need a daily fast of up to eighteen hours to thoroughly complete the task of digestion. Harvey Diamond, writer of the best seller, *Fit for Life,* describes our body cycles this way:

Noon to 8 P.M. APPROPRIATION (eating and digestion)
8 P.M. to 4 A.M. ASSIMILATION (absorbtion and use)
4 A.M. to noon ELIMINATION (body wastes & food debris)

Since so many Americans eat a hearty breakfast, a hearty lunch and a hearty dinner, far more time is spent *appropriating* than *eliminating.* No wonder 80 percent of us are overweight.

Action Step *Experience the benefits of fasting. Try to cut down on breakfast and soon you'll be able to skip it all together. We encourage you to drink special juices each morning. Start out with a glass of freshly extracted carrot juice and later have a glass of BarleyMax. Neither of these require any digestion. Remember the Father will reward you.*

Is There Dignity in Death?

I will praise the Lord as long as I live. I will sing praises to my God even with my dying breath.

—Psalm 146:2

Modern dying, for the most part, takes place in a hospital which does not have the amenities for proper goodbyes. Can there be such a thing as death with dignity? Dr. Sherwin Nuland, in his book *How We Die says,* "I have not often seen much dignity in the process by which we die."

He then goes on to describe the six medical "causes" of death—circulation stoppage, inadequate oxygen, flickering brain function, organ failure and destruction of the vital centers. I can understand why Dr. Nuland feels that the quest to achieve true dignity fails when our bodies fail. This "failure," however, is simply God's way of shutting down our earthly temple systems, getting us ready for a change of address in heaven.

Modern medicine is obligated to treat for survival and calm the pain with drugs. Too often our loved ones die in agony. But it wasn't so in the case of philosopher/theologian Francis Schaeffer.

Once he knew he was terminal, battling cancer, he visited each member of his family. His absent-from-the-body-present-with-the-Lord experience came at home while listening to his favorite music.

We all hope our lives end being surrounded with family and friends, singing and blessing and praying for one another. However, it is not death itself that is dignified. It is the ambiance preceeding death and the hope beyond death that can be made *dignified.*

Action Step *Thank God for life eternal. Talk about your death with your loved ones. Insure them that you have no fear of dying. Tell them you expect to bless them on the eve of your departure. Remind them that our enemy, death, has lost its power . . . its been swallowed up in victory.*

Sunshine: It's a Good Thing

Light is sweet; it's wonderful to see the sun.

—Ecclesiastes 11:12

Do you have mixed feelings about the sun? We've been taught that the sun is the secret of all life on planet earth. Yet we treat it as an enemy. We shield ourselves with parasols and sunglasses. But listen to this: "It is not possible for us to attain and sustain a full degree of health unless we establish and maintain an intelligent relationship with the sun." Harvey Diamond, *Fit for Life*.

Abundant sunshine is truly a source of many blessings . . .

- It helps us to lower our blood pressure.
- It lowers our blood sugar but increases our stress tolerance.
- It strengthens our immune system and draws toxins from the skin.
- It reduces our resting heart rate and cultivates a positive attitude.

These blessings of the sun are available through our skin and eyes. Yet most of us shun this powerful and essential energy by wearing sunscreen and sunglasses. We are fearful of the "damaging" effects of this heavenly star. In many cases this fear is, in one sense, well-founded. If a person is not in good health, the sun does burn and do damage.

So while we are taking steps to build our general health, we can initiate the following: Expose as much of the body as possible ten to fifteen minutes a day in the late afternoon. If you are a golfer or gardener with long periods in the sun, wear a wide brim hat as well as a light colored cotton shirt.

It makes no sense to have an aversion for the best friend mankind has. Enjoy the sun. It's beneficial.

> **Action Step** *Shine in me and through me, O Lord. Don't miss your daily quota of vitamin D and better calcium assimilation with a sunbath each day. You can exercise or weed your garden at the same time.*

Is There a Sinful Side to Eating?

If you are a big eater, put a knife to your throat, and don't desire the delicacies—deception may be involved.

—Proverbs 23:2

"Gluttony," wrote Billy Graham, "is one of the seven deadly sins and has been placed by the church fathers right alongside pride, envy and impurity. It is a sin that most of us commit, but few of us mention. It is one of the most prevalent sins among Christians."

Gluttony has always been seen from the beginning of time, but it only became widespread after the year 1900. The industrial revolution blossomed then with machinery both for the farmer and industrialist. For the first time in history the masses could purchase a large variety of foods. Not only the elite faced the temptation to overeat, but people in general could fall into the trap of eating too much.

Dr. Herbert Shelton headed up the *Natural Hygiene* movement from 1920 to 1960. In his last book he wrote that our eating is largely a matter of habit. He goes on saying that one of the worst eating habits is overeating. He felt that eating too much was universal. Is there a difference, he commented, between a man who kills himself with habitual gluttony or one who dies of alcohol?

Truly we are the most overfed, malnourished nation in the world. We may be living longer but real life and living has evaded many people. The current plague of chronic diseases have their roots in habitual gluttony. We eat too much, too often. We all practice temperance but rarely is it used to quell our indulgences with sweets, fats and salt. When a God-given normal hunger is extended, greedily, into gluttony, it harms the body, dulls the mind and stultifies the soul. This is sin.

Action Step *Work on a new appreciation for food. Confess the sin of over indulgence and ask for pardon. Always stop eating even before your stomach is full. Program a weekly fast. Rejoice in self-control.*

Does White Have a Dark Side?

"Come now, let us argue this out," says the Lord. "No matter how deep the stain of your sins, I can remove it . . . Even if you are stained as red as crimson, I can make you as white as wool."

—Isaiah 1:18

We all want to become clean, squeaky white and forgiven. But the analogy of whiteness stops here. The lack of color must be avoided if we are planning a menu that sparks vibrant health. There are five white foods we should stay clear of:

- *White sugar* is one of the most devastating man-made "foods" there is. The more one eats, the more you damage your body. If you need a sweetener, use honey or stevia.
- *White rice* has become popular the world over to the detriment of millions of people. The food processors polish off 40 percent of the key nutrients to make the rice white. Don't be fooled by the looks. Always insist on purchasing natural, brown rice.
- *White flour* products abound in the baked goods section of the supermarkets. Avoid them! Anyone who consistently consumes white bread, baked goods and most pastas will inevitability develop severe colon disease. Either grind the grain yourself or make sure the flour is whole. It is true—the whiter the bread, the sooner you are dead.
- *White salt* has been processed right out of the healthy category. What is done to the salt to make "it pour when it rains" is not to promote wellness. Use only sea salt. The best brand in the world comes from France—the brand name is Celtic Salt.
- *White lettuce* or pale green lettuce is the cheapest and most popular. It is also the least nutritious. When you buy organic lettuce, get the dark green Romaine, Greenleaf and Bibb.

Action Step *Be as white as you can inside but think rainbow as you fill your shopping cart. Look for the deep primary colors to enrich your salad bowl. Remember, if the food has been processed, the color you see is probably added and artificial.*

Disease Free, Incredible!

If you will listen carefully to the voice of the Lord your God and do what is right in his sight, obeying his commands and laws, then I will not make you suffer the diseases I sent on the Egyptians; for I am the Lord who heals you.
—Exodus 15:26

In 1971 they operated on my left shoulder. The melanoma lesion was removed by deep excision. Right after that, the first book I bought in my quest for health was *None of these Diseases* by S.I. McMillen M.D.. He felt that Exodus 15:26, written over 3,000 years ago, on how to avoid all sickness, can be just as true today. Naturally, the same conditions have to be fulfilled. They are: listen carefully to the Lord and obey His commands and laws.

What diseases did the Egyptians have? Paleopathologist Marc Ruffer autopsied many mummies and found they died of the same things that are killing us today. The degenerative conditions he found were: cancer, arthritis, emphysema, tuberculosis, etc. The Lord made it clear that the Israelites would have none of these diseases if they would follow closely His directions. Why can't the church of today heed this challenge?

Could the myriads of diseases that Jesus cured and our long list of terminal afflictions, be the consequences of disobedience? Could it be that by ignoring God's instructions, we Christians are as sick as the world is? However, in the last 100 years, we've begun to see how logical God's ancient health principles are. What could be more sensible than knowing which animals are OK to eat and which one are to be avoided. The Lord emphasized the importance of hand washing 3,500 years ago. A little over a century ago was the first time surgeons saw any need for it. It boils down to this; to the degree that we follow the Lord's rules of hygiene and diet—to that degree we'll be free of disease.

Action Step *Praise for this freedom. If you want to be totally well as I have been these past twelve years, you'll have to pay more attention to God's health principles and put them in practice.*

When Did We Ever See You Hungry?

And the king will tell them, "I assure you, when you did it to one of the least of these my brothers and sisters, you were doing it to me."
—Matthew 25:40

In spite of coming from humble roots, the Lord led Donna and me into the most challenging, the most important task in the world, being missionaries. At the time we signed up with the Latin America Mission, Donna was a primary school teacher and I was a veterinary pathologist working in cancer research with the USDA. Before going to Costa Rica to learn Spanish, we did our theological and missions training at the Moody Bible Institute.

Our new task, basically, was to fulfill the Great Commission. We were to plant a church where none had existed before. In doing so we encountered the *least of these*. The converts became like family to us. In these family circles we met those who needed clothes, the imprisoned, the hungry and the sick. Over the years it was the category of the *sick* that increased in number.

One main reason for this increase in chronic debilitation was the gradual switch from brown to white rice. Businessmen began buying up the newly harvested rice and polished it. It cost more but the Colombian women were delighted. They no longer had to pound it to get the chaff off, nor did they have to clean it. Furthermore, the cooking time was cut down. What they didn't realize was that 40 percent of the nutrients were lost in the polishing process. How much rice do the lowland Colombians eat?

Where we were working, near the Caribbean, over half of their diet was rice. No wonder we saw more ill people as time went on.

To the least of these we first showed them what was happening and then indicated how they could get natural brown rice like their grandparents had. Like Jesus, we preached the Gospel but also met their most obvious needs.

Action Step *We adore You for meeting our needs. There is more to feeding the sick than filling the stomach. Reach out to the least of these with answers to their urgent needs.*

The Health Titanic

Don't be impressed with your own wisdom. Instead, fear the Lord and turn your back on evil. Then you will gain renewed health and vitality.

—Proverbs 3:7

The look-out on the Titanic that saw the iceberg too late, only saw the tip— the one tenth above the water. Much of our *wisdom* is too often based on only what can be seen. Conventional medicine, for instance, operates mostly at the tip of the iceberg. Known also as Allopathic medicine, it focuses on and treats the obvious aspects of heart disease, cancer, diabetes and arthritis. These are really manifestations of deeper problems beneath the surface.

These nine tenths that are not seen are allergies, malabsorption, stress, hypoxia, insulin resistance, toxic overload, toxic dental fillings, nutrient deficiencies, obesity and hypothyroidism. These conditions are really the *cause* for most of the very visable symptoms.

The health practitioners that look below the surface to find the primary causes are the Chiropractors, the Naturopaths, the Homeopaths, the Doctors of Oriental Medicine and, of course, the new wave of Allopathic Doctors who have made the switch to Hollistic Medicine.

There is a basic flaw in our thinking about health care in this country. We treat symptoms rather than the underlying causes of disease. I was operated on several times, only to see the cancer come back. It was in a neighboring country that I finally found a therapy that could reverse the underlying cause of the melanoma cancer.

Action Step *Pray that the fear of the Lord be perfected. When you seek medical counsel, look for a practitioner who will take time to examine every aspect of your being—body, mind and soul. Don't be impressed with the high tech approach of attacking the symptoms. Seek to know the reason—the cause. Then, you are on the road to renewed health and vitality.*

Why Christians Get Sick

Don't copy the behavior and customs of this world; but let God transform you into a new person by changing the way you think. Then you will know what God wants you to do, and you will know how good and pleasing and perfect his will really is.

—Romans 12:2

Why? The Reverend George Malkmus needed to answer this question. He had officiated at the funerals of many cancer victims. His mother died of cancer and very soon afterward, he was diagnosed with colon cancer. How is it possible that those who are in the family of God suffer the same kind of diseases as those who have turned their backs on Him?

Pastor Malkmus found the answer in Romans 12:2. *To the degree that believers conform to the lifestyle of world, they will become as ill as non-believers.* And, to the degree that non-believers switch to the biblical, natural way of living and eating, they, too, will experience optimum health. A shocking truth!

"Is God to blame for sickness?" writes brother Malkmus. "I believe that it is high time we stopped hiding behind the Lord and blaming Him for, our physical problems. And that is exactly what we are doing by saying, "It is God's will when sickness comes."

George set out in a quest for *knowledge*. And that is what we all have to do. What Malkmus found was that most people ignore God's natural laws—the laws of physics and chemistry. Followers of Christ sincerely observe God's moral laws but gloss over God's secrets on how to live out the 120 healthy years He has given us.

The Lord expects us to breathe pure air. After all, 90 percent or more of our nutritional needs come from the air. God provided enough water. Today it is wise to purify the water we drink. Most of the food Jesus ate was whole, raw, living food. Examples of working to exercise leap from the pages of holy writ. Add to this sufficient exposure to the sun everyday, adequate rest and positive thinking for a balanced lifestyle.

Action Step *Don't copy the world any more. Get the book by Malkmus. Act on what you learn. Join us who follow God's natural laws.*

To Breathe Means Life

Then he said to me, "Speak to the winds and say: 'This is what the Sovereign Lord says: Come, O breath from the four winds! Breathe into these dead bodies so that they may live again.'"

—Ezekiel 37:9

We can live up to two months without eating. We can live several days without drinking, but less than five minutes without breathing. Since our lungs are so vital to life, it is no surprise that disease of the lungs is the fourth leading cause of death.

Chronic obstructive pulmonary disease (COPD) is a collective term for several lung diseases. Dr. Julian Whitaker, *Health & Healing*, September 2003, states that the most significant of all the COPD is emphysema.

Emphysema affects the alveoli where oxygen and carbon dioxide are exchanged. When these grape-like air sacs are damaged, less oxygen is extracted with each breath. To compensate, the lungs eventually enlarge and fill the entire lung cavity. This interferes with normal breathing, causing shortness of breath.

Conventional medicine says that there is *no* cure for emphysema.

It kills about 119,000 Americans each year, and sends another 726,000 to the hospital. This killer is managed with drugs, oxygen and surgery with little hope given.

Dr. Whitaker, however, says there is *hope*. They discovered success using the natural antioxidant **glutathione**.For COPD it has to be administered at home using a nebulizer directed into the lungs. This amazing free radical scanvenger liberates the airways.

Other products used in concert with the glutathione are vitamin C, N-acetyl-cysteine to break up mucus, magnesium to relax bronchioles and a high dose of vitamin A to help generate lung tissue.

Action Step *Shout His praises. Go to drwhitaker.com for further information. Share this good news with your physician. Thank the Lord for this breakthrough. It may save your life!*

A Thorn in the Flesh

But to keep me from getting puffed up, I was given a thorn in my flesh, . . . Three different times I begged the Lord to take it away . . . . For when I am weak, then I am strong.

—2 Corinthians 12:7–8,10

Do you have a "thorn" in your flesh? I do. I think mine has to do with allergies. Not only did I beg the Lord three times to take it away, I've been begging the Lord for over a year. I've even tried crying out to the Lord after reading Bill Gothard's *The Power of Crying Out.*

It's no fun to live with a runny nose and stuffed-up head. True, I do feel very well in spite of it. Could it be the same *grace* that Paul experienced that is giving me the victory? I think so.

Paul was a highly educated man. He no doubt experimented and did certain things to see if he could free himself from this thorn. I have also. First, I sent ten cubic centimeters of blood serum to an analytical lab. They said my problem was eggs. So I went without eggs for six months. Guess what? Nothing changed.

Next, I went on a non-wheat diet for weeks and guess what? My nose kept running. You won't believe this—I even tried drugs. I took a popular, over-the-counter allergy drug, just one pill. Guess what, it slowed the discharges a little but the next morning I could not urinate. It enlarged my prostate. So much for drugs.

The Bible says it and I believe it—*when I am weak, I am strong.* I told the Lord that it would be OK if I had to live the rest of my life with catarrhal discharges. Could this make my over-all ministry even stronger? I actually investigated another option I found in the field of Oriental Medicine but I'll tell you about that interesting venture another day.

Action Step *First, accept the thorn He has for you. Do what I did. I sent for the book* Breathe Again Naturally *by Bernard Jensen Ph.D. Discover that most respiratory conditions can be eliminated through nutrition. Pray that I discover the combination that works for me.*

Aerobics, We Need It

Remember that in a race everyone runs, but only one person gets the prize. All athletes practice strict self-control.

—1 Corinthians 9:24–25

Kenneth Cooper M.D. helped us to understand that we must exercise our heart and lungs by sustained movement at least three times a week. By sustained he meant bringing the heart rate up for periods of fifteen minutes. One can do this by jogging, swimming, cycling or working out on the treadmill.

My basic aerobic program is that of jogging three days a week and racewalking three days a week. I alternate. This has contributed greatly to my well-being. I am fit, trim and have the blood pressure of a young man. How do I keep motivated?

I compete. I stick to my aerobics program because I enter in the Senior Olympic Games of various counties. I race in the 1,500 meters racewalk, the 5 kilometers racewalk and the 1,500 meters run. I compete in the local games and I race at the level of the Florida State Championships. In 1999 I entered in the National Senior Games. I found out there were four men in this country that can beat me. Back then I was in the age bracket of seventy to seventy-four.

I have many gold medals in my collection as well as some silver ones. I won a bronze medal the only time I tried the long jump. The last time I competed in the games of my county, I won three gold medals. This is in the category of those who are seventy-five to seventy-nine years old. It is a lot of fun and I am motivated to stay in shape the year around. To the glory of God!

Cooper says that fitness is your platform for achieving your maximum potential in all aspects of life. Aerobics is one very key instrument in staying fit.

Action Step *Pray about how to get started. Get involved in the Senior Games in your area. Choose the sport such as running, swimming, cycling or racewalking that fill the requirements for aerobics. We all need it!*

The Perfect Exercise

For the Lamb who stands in front of the throne will be their Shepherd. He will lead them to the springs of life-giving water. And God will wipe away all their tears.
—Revelation 7:17

Having been given a prognosis of death in less than six months; we prayed. And the Lord led me to *the springs of life-giving water.* In three months I knew that the cancer was retreating. One factor in this natural therapy was, literally, *springs.* In this case it is specially designed springs that give the **Rebounder** the reputation of helping us in the perfect exercise.

One key to my rapid recovery and my tears being wiped away, was using the rebounder several times a day. It assisted in moving my toxic laden lymph more rapidly to my liver. This same detoxing was happening in every cell of my body. With each jump the cells squeeze out the waste and let in the life-giving oxygen. No wonder it was only a matter of weeks when I could no longer feel the tumurous lumps in my armpits.

A couple of positive things happen with each jump. At the top of each jump you are momentarily weightless. This is an instant of restfulness and it clears your mind. At the bottom of each jump one experiences two to four G Forces. The springs thrust you up with a force of two to four times your body weight. At this instant many benefits happen in your circulatory system. Waste matter, bacteria, cancer cells and dead cells are all flushed from your tissues.

The aerobic possibilities are another big plus. After warming up by simply jumping, one can begin to "run" by throwing the feet as far back as possible. Next you can thrust the feet forward. To really get the heart going I end my exercise session with lifting my knees belt-high as I do a running-in-place as long as I can.

Action Step *Jump for joy before the Lord. Think therapy and prevention. Get a Rebounder to make sure you avoid the killer diseases. Order your mini-trampoline(another name for Rebounder) from Hallelujah Acres. Exercising can be fun.*

Everything for God's Glory

Whatever you eat or drink or whatever you do, you must do all for the glory of God.

—1 Corinthians 10:31

The best explanation about the glory of God, is in Rick Warren's classic book *The Purpose Driven Life*. Chapter 7 is entitled *The Reason for Everything*. Rick sites Romans 11:36 as seen in the Living Bible: *Everything comes from God alone, everything lives by his power, and everything is for his glory.*

Warren goes on to explain: "The ultimate goal of the universe is to show the glory of God. Without God's glory there would be nothing. What is the glory of God? It is who God is. Where is the glory of God? Everything created by God reflects his glory—to the smallest form of microscopic life to the vast Milky Way, from sunset and stars to storms and seasons."

After God created everything and everyone, there was a rebellion caused by jealousy among the angels. Suddenly there was a negative force calling us for glory. Paganism became an option. We can think of ourselves as becoming New Age gods or we can show by every aspect of our life that all glory goes to our Creator.

The two most important things we do to sustain biological life are eating and drinking. According to our verse today, God must be glorified in our eating and drinking. Think how much it would change us if we took this seriously. We would have to evaluate all foods and drinks. Would they pass the test of being the quality our temples of the Holy Spirit require? Stewardship is a serious thing when we understand we are issued only one body. Only live foods build and repair the best. The more we can bring glory to God by what we eat and drink, the healthier we will be.

Action Step *Glory, glory, glory, from my whole being! Don't give taste top priority. Select what you eat and drink from the wide range of foods that God has provided for us. Beware of the man-made concoctions that fill the super-markets. Choose wisely that which gives energy to serve for the glory of God.*

A Good Example

Dear brothers and sisters, pattern your lives after mine, and learn from those who follow our example.

—Philippians 3:17

Our star example to follow is Jesus. The next biggest influence could be the apostle Paul. Today the group we look up to are those who faithfully practice biblical models. Who among us dare to say with Paul, "Do as I do"?

When Dr. David Frahm told what he was *doing*, he did not intimate that his readers should also do it. He simply responded to the repeated requests that he tell us what supplements he takes. So in the Health*Quarters* Monthly, January 2004, David briefly outlined what he takes to be assured of optimal health.

His example is important to the thousands who have been healed through his personal counsel. His sharing what he does also impacts the lives of those who have never met him, such as I, but have read his many books and regularly read the monthly.

His daily regimen has two aspects: first he fills the need of his detected deficiencies and then he supplements for ongoing protection and prevention. Through muscle testing he discovered that he is deficient in magnesium so he takes 2 capsules 3 times a day of Magnesium Malate. Then Frahm takes these to keep his organism finely tuned:

Thyroid . . . take Thyrostim, 2 caps 3 X a day with food, for gland health and stimulation.

Adrenals . . . take Spirulina, 2 caps 3 X a day with food, is restful for these overworked glands.

Liver . . . take Milk Thistle, 2 caps 3 X a day with food, detoxifies this important organ so intimately related to well-being.

Intestinal Tract . . . take Perfect 7, 1 tsp 2 X a day between meals.

This fiber blend cleans, detoxifies and regulates.

Action Step *Be aware of the many good examples in the Word of God. Don't be afraid to follow the example of those who do what they say. Praise God for those who walk the talk.*

Bad Food Produces Criminals

Get rid of all bitterness, rage, anger, harsh words, and slander, as well as all types of malicious behavior.

—Ephesians 4:31a

Can what people eat really affect the way they behave? The evidence says *yes*. Barbara Reed Stitt proved it and reports it in her book *Food & Behavior*. She worked for twenty years as a probational officer with a municipal court. Her job was to keep the ex-prisoners from becoming criminals once again. Usually, within three years, 80 percent are back in prison.

She began to ask the offenders about their diet because she had experienced a miraculous healing through changing the way she ate.

She describes the subjects assigned to her as being emotional wrecks who existed on donuts, pastries, white bread and all sorts of processed junk food. Instead of ordering the parolees to get appointments with a psychiatrist, she began to guide these hardened young men in the way they should eat.

Typically her program consisted of a simple diet of whole foods, eaten as fresh and unprocessed as possible. Coffee, soft drinks and milk were replaced with water and juices. The usual sugar-laden breakfast cereals were deleted for oatmeal. Dark green salads, fresh fruits and organically grown vegetables became the heart of the new diet.

Barbara has recommended dietary correction for thousands of probationers. Instead of 80 percent being arrested over and over again, over 80% changed into law-abiding citizens. They are living free and productive lives. A study was done analyzing hundreds of cases over a twelve year period. The report was that *not a single individual who stayed on the program had been back in trouble*.

The connection between diet and crime is an obvious fact.

Action Step *Thank God we are free. Ask about the strategy used by probation officers in your area. Pray about how the menu can be more of a factor in the prisons near you. Place the Reed Stitt book in the hands of key prison authorities.*

Fat or Fit

You have spent your years on earth in luxury, satisfying your every whim.
Now your hearts are nice and fat, ready for the slaughter.

—James 5:5

In many cases today, those who satisfy every whim not only have hearts crowded with fat, but also have obese bodies. According to the American Obesity Association 64.5 percent of Americans are overweight with half of them in the obese category.

Ready for the slaughter could mean that there are inevitable consequences since obesity is a major factor in diabetes, heart problems and various cancers. As many as 300,000 die each year from illnesses related to obesity.

"Obesity is by far the commonest single sign of physical unfitness in America," writes O.Q. Hyder M.D. in *Shape up.* "Next to sex, eating is the most satisfying of life's pleasures, but over indulgence leads to inexorable destructive effects." Dr. Hyder considers what a man weighs at 25 and a women at 18 is one's ideal weight for the rest their life. In my case this is true. At 25 I weighed 150 and now at 76 I weigh 150.

In my favorite weekly magazine, *WORLD*, issue 8.30.03, in the article *Why we are fat,* they observe that food serving sizes in restaurants have been growing. Years ago a soft drink contained just seven ounces. Now it contains twenty ounces. Even the pack of fries has tripled in size. With 30 percent of our meals eaten away from home, the larger serving portions have made us larger.

Dr. Hyder feels we need to look closer at Galatians 5:22,23. Temperance is one of the Fruits of the Spirit, but it seems to be unpopular with fat Christians. They'll condemn smoking and drinking but condone overeating.

Action Step *Hallelujah, there is a way. As keen stewards of our temples, cool the tendency to over indulge. Don't think of dieting as a deprivation of pleasure. Glorify God with a personality capable of discipline. Be fit!*

45

Stop That Fading Memory

But watch out! Be very careful never to forget what you have seen the Lord do for you. Do not let these things escape from your mind as long as you live.
—Deuteronomy 4:9

Since our brain is the master conductor of everything that goes on in the body, a sharp mind is a prerequisite to optimal health. Aging will slow our usual mental quickness but we are able to maintain a mental alertness and clarity as long as we live. If you want to, you can prevent ever being plagued with dementia or Alzheimer's.

In order to keep your brain healthy and sharp, you must protect it from free-radical damage. The brain contains more than 60 percent fat, a substance known to be highly sensitive to free radicals. Managing the stress in your life is the first step to slowing down damage, but nutrition plays a major role.

What is needed for most of us is a daily food supplement, an antioxidant, that nulifies free radicals. Also, the mixture needs to supply the nutrients the brain is crying for. These are the ingredients of a supplement that does the job:

- Vitamin E - Be sure to get the 4 kinds. It's an antioxidant.
- Gingo Biloba - It increases brain metabolism and blood flow.
- Coenzyme Q-10 - Helps produce cellular energy.
- Alpha Lipoic Acid - Regenerates E, C and glutathione.
- N-Acetyl-Cystiene - Stimulates the production of glutathione.
- Acetyl-L-Carnitine - Another aid to energy production in cells.
- Phosphatidylserine - Vital component for membranes of neurons.
- Essential Fatty Acids - Basic building blocks of neurons.
- Vitamin B complex - A sine qua non for the nervous system.

All these are found in *Brain Sustaine* formulated by Neurologist David Perlmutter. To prevent what happened to my Dad, I take it.

> **Action Step** *Praise Him with all your mind. Check out the website brainrecovery.com. Get the book. Do what you have to do to clearly remember in order to communicate the truth.*

An Answer to Cancer—CANTRON

But if you refuse to listen to the Lord your God and do not obey the commands and laws I am giving you today, all these curses will come and overwhelm you. The Lord will afflict you with the boils of Egypt and the tumors . . .
— Deuteronomy 28:15,27

People are dying from cancer *tumors* everyday. There were over 600,000 cancer deaths in 2002. Ed Sopak interviewed over 30,000 cancer patients and concluded that, "Traditionally accepted treatments are violent, irrational and the results are unacceptable."

Nine years ago an Oncologist told John Maras D.O. that he was terminal with two years to live. Maras went to the internet and ordered the product Cantron. He took one quarter teaspoon every four hours the clock around for several months. He is alive and well today with no sign of his prostate cancer that was killing him.

Dr. Maras soon found out that Cantron assists the body to rid itself of every kind of cancer.

This natural product was formulated by a chemist, the late James Vincent Sheridan in about 1936. He asked the Lord to give him a formula that would aid cancer patients. Since he recognized this as a gift from the Lord, he never wanted profit from it. To this day it is still non-profit.

Cantron is an antioxidant/electrolyte food supplement that lowers the electrical charge of the cancer cells. This forces the cells to ingest their own proteins. It weakens them to the point where the killer cells of the immune system can finish them off. Unlike chemo and radiation, there are no dreaded side effects.

Cantron works more rapidly and the patient agonizes less during healing crises, when the basics of the Hallelujah Diet are followed.

Action Step *Miracles are from You O Lord. Go to the website cantron.com for more details. You won't find the testimonies or what it is really capable of. For that you can contact me, Charles Miller in Lansing MI or Dr. Maras. Get the word out that there is hope. The whole therapy costs less than $200.*

It Seems Right

There is a path before each person that seems right, but it ends in death.
—Proverbs 14:12

Multiple sclerosis is a terrible disease. My close friend's son just died of it. In our local newspaper an MS patient wrote out her advice to those who relate to her. The point that caught my eye was, "Don't tell me about the latest fad cure. If there is a legitimate treatment, my doctor will let me know."

This *path* to her seemed *right*. But how do you think it will end? Over 3,000 die of MS in this country every year. I'm glad she has confidence in her doctor. I'm sad that she is not aware of his limitations. No one knows it all. Her doctor knows what he knows but is he open minded enough to admit that there could be answers he does not know about.

Thirteen years ago my Oncologist *knew* that I would die of melanoma within six months. Science was on his side. He told me that all of his metastatic melanoma patients in the past had died within six months. I put his suggested protocol on hold while I prayerfully looked literally to the ends of the earth for options. It was in March of 1991 that I focused on the Gerson Therapy in Mexico.

What makes anything legitimate? I've read testimonials of MS patients that I believe are legitimate. The publishers are responsible people. These patients had suffered for years—were confined to wheelchairs. Now they are so improved that they are back to part time work.

Not everything that seems right ends in death. In these cases what seemed right for them was the Hallelujah Diet or Hyperbaric Oxygen Therapy or even the Cantron Wellness program. What has been accepted in the past as a picture of progressive morbidity, can now be changed with a cautious prognosis of possible reversal.

> **Action Step** *O Lord, show me the path. Don't be afraid to switch to another path, it could save your life.*

48

Use Your Family Tree

When Herod died, an angel of the Lord appeared to Joseph in Egypt and told him, "Get up and take the child and his mother back to the land of Israel . . ."
—Matthew 2:19–20

This Herod that killed all the boy babies of Bethlehem and died soon afterward, is the first of four generations of Herods. In *The Open Bible* published by Thomas Nelson, a family tree of the Herods appears on page 1338. This is very helpful.

One of the most fascinating books I ever read on health featured the family tree. Chris Reading M.D. entitled his book *Trace Your Genes to Health.* Dr. Reading is convinced that most of the ills that beset us can be diagnosed, predicted and even prevented. All this by just studying the family tree. He declares that many of our worst diseases are frequently transmitted genetically.

Bernard, a top executive, was checked by eight specialists who sought the reasons for his severe symptoms of losing his speech and balance. He could barely write and suffered from blinding headaches. All the diagnostic tests proved negative. He was finally referred to Dr. Reading.

By carefully mapping out the family tree *medical* history of four generations, it quickly became clear to Dr. Reading what the problem was. The key clue was noting who had received the color blind X chromosome. The diagnosis was *celiac disease* caused by massive allergies to grains.

This in turn caused a severe vitamin/mineral deficiency which triggered an autoimmune response. The treatment consisted of a totally grain-free diet and heavy doses of the vitamins and minerals he was low on. After suffering many years, now Bernard was symptom free. He got his life back—thanks to the study of his family tree by a professional who knew what genetics is all about.

***

Action Step *Open your mind to new dimensions of diagnosis. Get the book and use your medical family tree for guidance in diet and overcoming chronic disease.*

Who Will See the End?

I assure you, this generation will not pass from the scene before all these things take place.

—Matthew 24:34

What *things* was Jesus referring to? From verse 4 through 31 Jesus describes the tribulation and the second coming. The next logical question would be, what *generation* is Jesus talking about?

Of all that has been written about the end-times, Charles Miller's book, *Today's Technology in Bible Prophesy* is the clearest to me. He points out who it is that will see it all—atomic World War I, one world government, the antichrist, the great tribulation, the rapture, atomic World War II and Jesus' return to the earth.

Miller is sure that Zechariah's vision of a manned space flight initiates the time of the *final* generation. Who are they? Everyone who was 19 years old or younger on April 12, 1961. It was on that date that the Russian Yuri Gagarin was the first to circle the globe in space.

Miller goes on to observe that the healthiest of mankind live about 100 years. He considers it the time of one generation. Theoretically, if one were ten years old in April 1961, and lives 100 years, by the year 2051 he will have seen all of what Jesus called the END.

What I've just reported to you in 200 plus words, Miller takes 500 pages to give in great detail the fate of Iraq, China, and Israel and just how it will all end. He challenges the reader to be prepared both *physically* and spiritually for the coming chaos on earth. Knowing that these catastrophic events are about to happen and being alerted to the soon coming of nuclear holocausts, we should be motivated to be our best.

Action Step *Come quickly, Lord Jesus! Get the book to check these things out for yourself. Let's face the end-time events with a faith and a physique that is fit and trim. See how the prophets of old had visions of today's technology but had an ancient vocabulary to work with. What an eye-opener.*

Salt, Are You Worth It?

You are the salt of the earth, but what good is salt if it has lost its flavor?
—Matthew 5:13

How important is salt, especially if you and I are to be *the salt of the earth?* The truth is salt is very important. Without the sodium of salt we would die. It is the primary stabilizing factor of the fluids between all our cells. And the chloride of salt is used by the body to make the hydrochloric acid in the stomach for breaking down what we eat.

The problem today is that we have become addicted to the taste of salt. We like it so much that we eat about ten times the amount we need. In doing so, the excess sodium forces its way into the cells where potassium rules as an alkalizer. This upsets the cellular balance so badly that the cells malfunction.

The resulting disease manifestations range all the way from high blood pressure to cancer. It is good advice to cut down on salt intake. But don't go to the other extreme. Look at this case reported in the IBLP Newsletter of Bill Gothard, June 2003.

"We came to this seminar hoping to get help for our daughter Janell who has fibromyalgia. She was so ill that she vomited for five days. We were desperate. On the first night of the conference Dr. Roger Billica mentioned the importance of having salt in our diet.

Janell had been on a no-salt diet for months. After the meeting we met with Dr. Billica. He advised us to give Janell one teaspoon of sea salt in a glass of water every other day. A few hours after the first salt drink, the pain in her legs began to leave. By the next day her acid reflux was gone. We praise God for this marvelous healing."

Action Step *Lord, don't let me lose my flavor. Avoid the ordinary, over processed table salt with its aluminum compounds. Get Celtic salt which comes from Brittany, France and contains trace minerals as well. It's the best in the world.*

Take Control

But Jesus said, "It must be done, because we must do everything that is right."
—Matthew 3:15

Yes, we are to take charge of our health—it is the right thing to do. T.C. Fry said it very "up front;" health care is self care.

"It's a totally do-it-yourself affair for humans as it is for animals in nature. No one can breathe for you, drink for you, eat for you, exercise for you or sleep for you. It's what *you* do that establishes the condition for personal well-being."

The health care industry in the US is currently more than a one billion-dollar-a-year business. Unfortunately, most of this money is spent on repair rather than on prevention. In other words, on treating illness rather than helping people learn how to stay well. This no doubt reflects the fact that medical doctors get very little training in nutrition and prevention of disease.

Our body is our responsibility. We are only issued one of them for this lifetime. Let's not be like the lady who after telling the doctor her aches and pains, screams out, "Doctor, do something." She evidently did a lot of things wrong and now expects the doctor to undo them. This idea of looking to a doctor to "fix it" is quite prevalent. It's basically saying that one is not responsible for what happens to one's body but the doctor is now asked to repair it.

Jesus taught that we must do what is right. To be responsible is the right thing. And we should begin before a major crisis happens.

For instance, we know that half the people who suffer a heart attack never reach the hospital alive. It's much easier to prevent a killer disease before it happens than to regain your health once it has done so much damage. Death is difficult to reverse.

Solomon reminds us that wisdom will multiply our days and add years to our life. Good health does not come easily—it takes work. The more you take charge, the healthier you will be.

Action Step *Subscribe to some wellness newsletters. Get monthly input to choose from in taking charge.*

Permaculture

Then God said, "Let the land burst forth with every sort of grass and seed-bearing plant. And let there be trees that grow seed-bearing fruit." . . . This all happened the third day.

—Genesis 1:11–13

When God created all the plant life, He had food in mind. Man organized nature into what we call agriculture. When the thinkers of the past generation saw how modern agriculture was depleting rapidly our natural resources, they put together a system of food production that was *sustainable*. They called it *permaculture* because it could sustain itself permanently.

Even after the Fall, when nature was invaded by what we call weeds, the soil was capable of renovating itself naturally. The Israelites followed instructions given by the Lord and allowed their land to "rest" every seven years to maintain fertility. My grandfather followed the farming practice of rotating the crops as well as allowing the land to "fallow" or rest every five years. Today, however, land is exploited to the utmost, year after year. The permaculture people don't like it.

Permaculture is based on cooperating with nature and at the same time producing all the organic food needed. One of the local permaculture families is Johnny Papaya Burns and his wife Nati.

Rather than living on a farm they live in the heart of the city Sarasota, Florida. They have a pie-shaped lot on a cul-de-sac. It's hard to believe unless you see it. There is not one blade of grass on their whole lot. Rather it is alive with plants, trees and bushes all of which produce food.

The genius of permaculture is to have food producing crops at seven levels. The Burns have trees of different heights, bushes at various levels, and plants that give food above and below the earth.

Most of what they eat, they themselves grow. Johnny and Natividad are the healthiest people in town.

Action Step *Be a blessing by making everything you do more sustainable. Do it as good stewards.*

The Money Changers

In the temple area he saw merchants selling cattle, sheep and doves for sacrifices; and he saw money changers behind their counters. Jesus made a whip from some ropes and chased them all out of the temple . . . he told them, "Get these things out of here. Don't turn my father's house into a marketplace!"
—John 2:14–16

My fellow Health Minister, Greg Schumacher, shared with the whole Hallelujah Diet family what he believed the story of Jesus' cleaning out the temple is saying today. He said it this way:

"Knowing that our bodies are the temple of God, how do I view this passage? Friends, the food, medical and pharmaceutical industries are the money changers who are buying and selling inside of our bodies. They are making huge profits inside the body/temple at our expense.

"Jesus said, 'Is it written, My house will be called a house of prayer for all nations. But you have made it a den of robbers." Jesus also said, "How dare you make my father's house into a market!' Our bodies are to be a house of prayer, not a marketplace for big business. So many of us are suffering so much from the effects of the money changers that we can hardly pray for anything except the illnesses of our friends, our family and ourselves.

"We are too tired and miserable to be effective for the Lord. Our own bodies have become a den of robbers as these money changers ply their addictive wares and poisonous lies inside of us. Jesus is throwing them out using a special whip. And that whip is our leader, Rev. George Malkmus and all of us Health Ministers, to restore His temple to a house of prayer. The Hallelujah Diet and natural healing are restoring life to our body/temples, which are sacred and are the 'Most Holy Place.'" Thank you, Greg, for that enlightening insight.

Action Step *Be a part of the whip in Jesus' hand. Kindly help others in the cleansing process. Pray constantly.*

Our Incredible Immune System

In the thirty-ninth year of his reign, Asa developed a serious foot disease. Even when the disease became life threatening, he did not seek the Lord's help but sought help only from his physicians. So he died in the forty-first year of his reign.

—2 Chronicles 16:12–13

Death is inevitable but the reason we live as long as we do is because of our incredible immune system. It is complex, intricate and interesting. It's an amazing protection mechanism. It defends us against millions of bacteria, viruses, toxins and parasites that would love to invade us. To understand the power of the immune system, all we have to do is to look at what happens to any creature once it dies.

That sounds gross, but it does show us something very important about our system. When a living organism dies its immune system (along with everything else) shuts down. In a matter of hours the body is invaded by all sorts of microbes, none of which were able to get in when the immune system was working.

But the moment the immune system stopped working, every door went open. Once a creature or a person dies, it only takes a few weeks for the microbes to completely dismantle the body and carry it away, until all that's left is a skeleton. Obviously the immune system is doing something amazing to keep all the dismantling from happening when the person is alive.

Actually, King Asa did over three milennia ago what most do today—go to the doctor. Today's scripture gives another option—go to the Lord, and maybe not die. The Lord reminds us that He has equipped us with a marvelous defense system. All we have to do is cooperate with it by feeding it living food, furnish it with an abundance of pure water, get some of His sun and breathe in a lot of oxygen He surrounds us with. Asa died saturated with medicines. You and I can live a long and vibrant life by knowing how to work with our God-given immune systems.

Action Step *Enhance your immune system daily by taking the antioxidants alpha lipoic acid, grape seed extract and co-Q-10.*

George Washington: Medical Martyr

Remain faithful even when facing death, and I will give you the crown of life.
—Revelation 2:10b

On December 13, 1799 George Washington summoned his doctor after coming down with a sore throat. His doctor bled him four times, injected him with poisonous mercury, gave him more mercury by mouth, then blistered his throat with a compound of vinegar and dead bugs. After enduring this torturous treatment for a single day, the father of our country begged his doctor to leave him alone and let him die in peace. President Washington died at 10 P.M. on December 14.

"Your good health is far too precious to be entrusted solely to doctors," wrote Charles Kennedy M.D. in a Mayo Clinic Letter. He went on to say why; "An informed person, when equipped with the up-to-date knowledge of what's happening in the ever-changing world of medicine, can form an intelligent partnership with me that will make my efforts more effective."

I read some of "what's happening" in medicine today in the December 2003 issue of *Health Freedom News*. The article is entitled "American Medicine Now the Leading Cause of U.S. Deaths." The Nutritional Institute of America headed by Gary Null Ph.D. announced their research findings on October 28, 2003 that the projected death toll from medical errors is 783,936 per year. This displaces heart disease (669,697) as the nation's top killer. Cancer is now in third place with 553,251 deaths annually.

The fatalities caused by medical errors are called "iatrogenic deaths." It actually means "doctor caused." Post surgery complications alone cause 32,000 deaths a year. Most of the deaths are caused by adverse *drug* reactions. My aunt's prescription was changed and within 24 hours she reacted violently and became a "vegetable." She died six months later.

Action Step *Do all you can to stay out of the hospital. Seek out a natural remedy before you ask for a drug. If sick—fast!*

The Staff of Life

Give us our food for today, and forgive us our sins . . .

—Matthew 6:11

Jesus knew that healthy food had to be prepared *daily*. God confirmed the necessity of daily dependence by designing manna that would last only one day except the seventh day. All bread was prepared and baked everyday for thousands of years. But a little over a hundred years ago, the industrial revolution caught up with grinding wheat into flour. Steel roller mills changed breadmaking from a local, fresh, natural industry to vast nationwide monopoly. It also changed the "Staff of Life" into the "scythe of death." The high speed roller milling raises the temperature and furiously wipes out the key ingredients that makes bread so good.

The bran, the endosperm and the wheat germ are removed because the natural oils begin to turn rancid very soon after the protective hull is cracked. In the same way that God designed manna to self destruct at the end of the day, He created wheat to deteriorate rapidly once it has been milled. We'll not get the full nutritional benefit unless the bread is made soon after the flour is milled.

To do it yourself you need a stone grinder, organic grains, pure water, sea salt, an oven *and* natural leavening instead of brewer's yeast. The beer industry's yeast makes the bread rise but does not clear the dough of the dangerous *phytin* in grains that binds up minerals and prevents their absorption. Genuine leavening, on the other hand, is where a variety of microbes such as bacteria, fungi and yeasts "digests" the phytic acid in the dough.

The options are obvious, either mill the grain into flour yourself or purchase bread from a bakery that grinds daily. We were delighted to find such a bakery in Roswell, Georgia. But suddenly it moved to another city. My daughter then bought her own mill.

We began buying a very special bread at the health store. It is called Ezekiel 4:9 bread. We keep it frozen—it's so good.

Action Step *When you ask God for daily bread, don't be satisfied with something less. Keep life in the Staff of Life.*

Change the Food, Change the Child

This same good news that came to you is going out all over the world. It is changing lives everywhere, just as it changed yours . . .

—Colossians 1:6a

Concerned parents looked for a way to change what was going on at Appleton Central Alternative High School in Wisconsin.

The school was out of control. Kids packed weapons. Discipline problems swamped the principal's office. Dropouts were way too high. Kids were expelled and others committed suicide.

What did parents do? Did they bring in more cops? Did they install a metal detector? No. They invited a local health food firm, National Ovens Bakery, to prepare *healthy lunches*. Out went the greasy fast food and in came a spa-like salad bar along with great whole-grain bread. Out went all the vending machines and in came fresh fruits and *pure water.*

The change was like from night to day. Grades are up and truancy is no longer a problem. Fights and arguments are rare and teachers are able to spend more time teaching. After two years there were no more dropouts, no more suicides and no more expulsions. One teacher had decided to quit but after seeing the incredible change, decided to continue to teach.

What a concept—eating healthier food increases concentration.

Students talked about it. "I admit," said one student, "I sorta miss the burgers and fries but with the new food I can concentrate and get along with people." Change will only happen when parents take the initiative. Big corporations are constantly knocking at the door of the school board offering them thousands of dollars. All they want is the green light to once again line the corridors with vending machines. Be it in your home, church or school, changing the food will change the child.

Action Step *Get involved in your school system. Step into the battle—stand up and be counted. Save the children with the right food. Begin to change lives everywhere, starting at home.*

You Are Not Sick, You Are Thirsty

You must serve only the Lord your God. If you do, I will bless you with food and water, and I will keep you healthy.

—Exodus 23:25

We've taken water for granted but it is a major player in life. In spite of being shown how important water is, time after time, it never got through to me until I read the book *Your Body's Many Cries for Water* by F. Batmanghelidj M.D. The story behind this man is interesting.

Some years ago when Iran had a major revolution, Dr. Batman, along with hundreds of other professionals, were jailed to await execution. Because they needed a doctor in the prison, they stayed his being put to death. He was told to treat the sick but was given no medicine. He was forced to use water as treatment. He did it scientifically and had marvelous results.

He avoided having his head cut off and eventually escaped to the U.S. with his notes. This book I refered to above came out in 1992. He calls it "A Preventive and Self-Education Manual" for those who prefer to adhere to the logic of the natural and simple medicine. Over and over he pleads with us not to *treat thirst with* medicine.

Dehydration (lack of water) manifests itself in so many ways. We are sure we are coming down with heart disease, pneumonia, a cold, arthritis, cancer, another migraine, etc. And all the time it is really just dehydration. Even bulimia is a complication of severe dehydration.

Even though water is needed in digestion, do not drink during the meal. Rather take a large glass thirty minutes before you eat and little or no liquids during the meal and all will go well. And not drink again until your stomach is almost empty. That is some two and one half hours after a meal.

Action Step *Don't count other liquids as part of your eight-glass quota of water each day. Go to watercure.com and order the book. The most important health decision is to drink more aqua(water).*

A Different Approach to Allergies

Thank you for making me so wonderfully complex! Your workmanship is marvelous—and how well I know it.

—Psalm 139:14

There is archeological evidence that the Chinese began to describe certain marvels of the human body 5,000 years ago, what today we call acupuncture points. This was not that many generations removed from the great flood of Noah's time. Surely the offspring of Noah knew something of the wonders of the body.

Young Devi Nambudripad, whose parents had come to Los Angeles from India, was a very sick little girl. So she dreamed of studying medicine to find the cause of her many allergies. She began her medical training at the L.A. College of Chiropractic. At this college she was exposed to Oriental Medicine and acupuncture.

In time she took classes at an acupuncture college where she learned about kinesiology and muscle testing. She mastered it.

She learned she was allergic to all foods except white rice and broccoli and as long as she only ate these, life was bearable. The challenge before her was that of overcoming completely these hundreds of allergies. With the use of acupuncture she accidently discovered how to, get this, *reprogram* the brain so it would no longer call good food an enemy and start an allergic reaction.

We know that every object on earth, whether living or non-living, has an energy field around it. By using muscle testing, the practitioner can find out what the allergens are. The patient then holds the suspected allergen in her hand while the clinician inserts needles at the appropriate acupuncture points. The treatment lasts less than thirty minutes. But effectively the "blockage" is gone and the brain will never again give an allergic reaction to whatever she had in her hand during the treatment.

Action Step *Go to Dr. Devi's web site naet.com and find out who has been training to do the Nambudripad's Allergy Elimination Technology in your area. Get her book also.*

Cup of Demons

You cannot drink from the cup of the Lord and from the cup of demons, too.
—1 Corinthians 10:21

When I opt to "pay inside" for the gasoline I pump, as I open the front door of the store, I am confronted with piles of stacked cases of drinks—colas, sport drinks and beer. *Who buys all this?* I'm thinking. But watching people leave, I see that 90 percent either have a bottle in their hand or are carrying a case out. If it's not water, could it be a *cup of demons?*

The average American guzzles down fifty-six gallons of soft drinks each year. The real dangers of soda-pop can be seen as we review the ingredients. Let's take a look at the components of a can of soda: *Sugar: One can of soda has about ten teaspoons of sugar. It increases insulin levels and this leads to higher blood pressure, higher cholesterol, diabetes, weight gain and heart disease. *Phosphoric Acid: It interferes with the body's handling of calcium.

Girls that drink cola beverages have nearly five times the risk of bone fracture over those who drink very little. This acid also neutralizes the hydrochloric acid in the stomach, interfering with digestion. *Aspartame: This chemical is used as a sugar substitute. There have been ninety-two negative health side effects cataloged in the use of aspartame. Some of them are brain tumors, birth defects, diabetes, emotional disorders and epilepsy.

*Caffeine: This ingredient causes the jitters, insomnia, high blood pressure, irregular heart beat, vitamin and mineral depletion and elevated blood cholesterol levels. The excessive consumption of soft drinks in this country has to be a major contributor to poor health. It leaves you with little appetite for the good food—the fruits and vegetables your body cries out for. We've got to choose between the cup of the Lord or the cup of demons.

Action Step *Break the habit of drinking anything other than pure water. Go to the web, mercola.com, for related material.*

Juice, the Best Fast Food

I was holding Pharaoh's wine cup in my hand, so I took the grapes and squeezed the juice into it.

—Genesis 40:11

Rather than do as Pharaoh's cup-bearer did, squeezing fruit, the advice today is juice your vegetables and eat your fruit.

One of the first to teach juicing was Dr. N.W. Walker. His fascinating book *Raw Vegetable Juices* was printed in 1936 and the 1967 version sold for $2. He clearly explains the rational for separating the juice from the fiber. After all, most of the nourishment of a vegetable is in the juice. The body can assimilate the juice in ten minutes. But eating the whole vegetable could require two hours for digestion and spend a lot of energy doing it.

"Drinking the freshly-extracted juices of vegetables is the fastest way to obtain the nutrients necessary to restore the body to health," so writes Michael Dye in *God's Way to Ultimate Health*. He goes on to explain that our living body cells require living, whole nutrients from living vegetables. Drinking freshly extracted juice from fresh raw vegetables is the ultimate in nutrition. It is true that one could eat the raw carrot and get the same good out of it. But who is going to chew down a pound of raw carrots in order to get six ounces of juice you want?

To combat any condition or illness, it makes sense to serve the body with concentrated nutrients. And the best source of cellular food is freshly extracted juice. Because the fiber has been removed, the fresh living nutrients in the juice can get into the bloodstream and to the cellular level in minutes, without the time-consuming and energy-depleting process of digestion. The appliance needed for juicing is an extractor. Be sure to get the kind that will render the best juice. Organic carrot juice in combination with apple and celery are good for any condition. Be sure to sip slowly and let the saliva mix well with the juice.

Action Step *Extract the juices in your own kitchen. Contact Hallelujah Acres for the right kind of extractor.*

To the Ends of the World

Then Jesus said to the Roman officer, "Go on home. What you have believed has happened." And the young servant was healed that same hour.

—Matthew 8:13

Medicine, clinics and hospitals have had an important role in worldwide evangelism for more than a century. One of the best analysis of medical ministry that I know of was written by veteran missionary Daniel E. Fountain, M.D. He was asked by the Billy Graham Center to write a monograph on biblical perspectives on health and healing. He entitled his book *Health, the Bible and the Church.*

Using his thirty years of medical missionary experience in Africa, Dr. Fountain developed a theology of human wellness that in some ways rebukes his own profession. At the same time he summons churches to recover their rightful role as partners with physicians.

The heart of this excellent study is the *whole person.* He reminds us that the *WHOLE* includes body, mind and spirit. They are inseparable, interrelated, interdependent and "intermingled." For instance, resentment can cause blood pressure changes, peptic secretions and intestinal activity.

Therefore healing must be oriented toward the restitution of the whole person in the total context of relationships. What good was it for Dr. Fountain to purge a whole village of hook worms when six months later they would again be totally infested with these parasites? Without a previous orientation on the biology of the hook worm, sanitation, parental responsibility and the fear of God, medicine in itself proved to be worthless.

Health is a moral issue also. Since we are accountable to God for the use of our body, mind and spirit, it is wrong to do anything that harms them. In fact, Fountain extends the accountability to oneself and others. Food abuse, neglect of personal hygiene and poor physical fitness are health issues and moral questions as well.

Action Step *Get this book. Missions will make more sense than ever. Add these new insights to your leadership role.*

Dem Bones, Dem Dry Bones

Then he said to me, "Speak to these bones and say, 'Dry bones, listen to the word of the Lord! This is what the Sovereign Lord says: Look! I am going to breathe into you and make you live again!'"

—Ezekiel 37:4–5

When our bones become dry, it'll take more than breathing into them for restoration. At the same time it is good to see what the *Sovereign Lord* may choose to reveal to us today. Calcium is still what good bones are all about. Calcium is important for optimal health. More calcium supplements are sold than any other mineral.

There is a good reason—there is more calcium in the body than all the other minerals added together.

It is needed for strong bones and teeth. It maintains our heartbeat evenly and is basic to the transmission of nerve impulses.

It helps to keep the skin healthy and guards pregnancies. On the other hand, a deficiency can contribute to osteoporosis, insomnia, hypertension, kidney stones and colon cancer.

The best sources of calcium are plant foods such as organic lettuce, kale, spinach, most vegetables and beans along with fresh fruit. Best to avoid soft drinks because they pick up calcium and dump it into the urine.

The best calcium supplement is calcium lactate because it is only one step from the ionized form that the body can assimilate. To be sure that your calcium level is always where in should be, get the supplement *Ipriflavone*. Take 200 mg three times a day with meals. Too often our body runs short of this marvelous calcium regulator that plays a key role in every step of bone formation. With Ipriflavone, your calcium worries are over. But there is one more supplement needed—*L-Lysine* helps greatly in calcium absorption.

> **Action Step** *Increase your intake of fresh, living greens. Add to your daily regimen of supplements: L-Lysine, calcium lactate and Ipriflavone. Help your bones live again!*

The Common Cold

When Jesus arrived at Peter's house, Peter's mother-in-law was in bed with a high fever. But when Jesus touched her hand, the fever left her. Then she got up and prepared a meal for him.

—Matthew 8:14–15

It's good to touch base with Jesus at the first sign of developing a cold. Most likely He will not "touch" your cold away but will help you to remember what you are about to read.

The average adult has two or more colds a year and in total they spend over a billion dollars a year on non-prescription remedies. A lot of studies have been done on the common cold. One at USCC found out that those who have a moderate to high level of physical activity experienced 25 percent fewer colds. Taking a thirty-minute walk each day will reduce the risk considerably.

There are over two hundred viruses that can cause the common cold. Is this the reason for the fact that there is *no cure*? But there are several things one can do to reduce the length of the cold. The first is to take zinc-acetate lozenges within twenty-four hours of the onset of the cold symptoms. In a study those that took zinc had a cold for five days while those who took a placebo had their colds for eight days.

Also at the first sign of a cold, take an alcohol-free echinacea and goldenseal combination extract to boost your immune system and keep the virus from multiplying.

Other wise recommendations are: Add garlic and ginger to your meals. Take 500 mg of L-lysine daily to aid in destroying the viruses and prevent cold sores. Drink more water than usual and sip hot turkey or chicken broth. Wash your hands often and remember that antibiotics are useless against viruses. Avoid remedies that contain the dangerous diphenhydramine.

Action Step *Welcome a brief high fever—it's helpful. Stay as active as possible. Take 1,000 mg of vitamin C every 2 hours during the day. Shoot for the goal of zero colds this year.*

An Astounding Story

Bend down, O Lord, and hear my prayer; answer me, for I need your help.
—Psalm 86:1

William D. Kelly DDS was practicing orthodontics. In 1963 he started to feel ill. He continued to deteriorate and suffer for three years. He was finally diagnosed with liver and pancreatic cancer that was inoperable. The prognosis was death within two months.

As a convinced and practicing Christian, he prayed, maybe the same words seen above. Kelly admitted that for some years he had noticed that the scriptures did lay out basic dietary "laws." So the first thing he did was change, radically, what he ate and drank. He became a vegetarian and drank a quart of freshly extracted carrot juice each day. Fresh raw fruit or their juice were a daily menu item. At both lunch and dinner he had a fresh raw salad. His breakfast was a mixture of raw whole-grain cereals. He would grind the amount for a meal and cover it with water overnight. In the morning he would add some honey and fruit before enjoying it.

The two months came and went. Kelly sensed he was winning even though he was in bad shape. He not only had to destroy the cancer, but had to rebuild a badly shattered body. Along with this strict dietary regimen, Kelly had all the silver fillings taken out of his mouth and replaced with gold to avoid possible mercury toxicity. Furthermore, he supplemented with the best pancreatic enzymes he could get. This is based on the known observation that pancreatic enzymes do digest the cancer cells if there is enough potent exposure.

Once Kelly recovered, hundreds of "terminal" patients were referred to him by other physicians. In his book *One Answer to Cancer* he tells how he counseled thousands of dying patients and saw the majority reverse cancer and get totally well.

Action Step *Note how the same basic nutritional therapy laws are repeated in all good programs. Be glad that you are understanding these facets of truth.*

A Young Heart

As pressure and stress bear down on me, I find joy in your commands. Your decrees are always fair; help me to understand them, that I may live.

—Psalm 119:143–144

Pressure and stress as well as age are hard on hearts. But there is good news. As usual the experiments start in a lab. Scientists at the Linus Pauling Institute measured DNA damage in the hearts of older rats that were near their death. They found that old hearts produce three times more free radicals than young hearts.

The scientists gave the old rats *alpha lipoic acid* just two weeks before they were expected to die. The investigators were surprised to find that the heart muscle cells of the old rats now gave off no more free radicals than did the hearts of the young, unsupplemented rats. This rejuvenation effect on the heart has now been substantiated on humans. A closer look at alpha lipoic acid helps us understand why it makes old hearts young again.

The genious of lipoic acid is based on the fact that it is another phenomenol antioxidant. And that's not all. It works within the membranes of the cells and in the intracellular plasma. There it has the ability to actually regenerate vitamin E and glutathione so they can be used time and time again. This unusual acid has been shown to also help in the transport of glucose. Diabetics appreciate that. Another study showed how alpha lipoic acid prevented and in some cases stopped the formation of cataracts.

Few diseases are as devastating as Alzheimer's. There is no cure. But doctors in Germany gave 600 mg of lipoic acid each day to patients recently diagnosed with Alzheimer's. The immediate effect was stabilization to the point where they experienced no more loss of their cognitive function. Praise the Lord! Can you see why I have decided to take alpha lipoic acid the rest of my life?

Action Step *Take 300 mg of alpha lipoic acid twice a day with meals if you are trying to overcome something. Take it once a day for prevention and energy. Keep your heart young!*

Healing the Hopeless

Moved with pitty, Jesus touched him. "I want to," he said. "Be healed!" Instantly the leprosy disappeared—the man was healed.

—Mark 1: 41,42

Leprosy was considered hopeless 2,000 years ago. By curing all diseases and even death, Jesus substantiated His divinity. In 1881 two jews were born in Germany, Einstein and Gerson. Both ended their lives in the USA. Einstein revolutionized physics. Gerson came up with the underlying principles behind the causes and effects of good and ill health.

He developed the concept of totality in medicine that later became known as holism or wholistic medicine. Like Einstein, Gerson was attacked by many of his colleagues. But according to Albert Schweitzer, Gerson was one of the most eminent geniuses in the history of medicine. Max Gerson M.D. became known as one who cured the *incurables*. I looked for his clinic in 1991 when I was told I was *terminal* with metastatic melanoma cancer. I found it in Mexico.

Gerson's healing the hopeless started during med school when he was suffering with migraines. His professors informed him that migraines were incurable. So he experimented with nutrition and cured himself. Among the hundreds that came to him to be cured of migraines, several were also cured of what was killing thousands—tuberculosis. After escaping Hitler's holocaust and coming to the US, he was called on to cure many who were dying of cancer.

He saved many lives on juices, coffee enemas, and garlic and flax seed oil. Florida senator, Claude Pepper, called Gerson in for cancer hearings. He came with five recovered terminal cancer cases.

At this point the AMA and the FDA declared all out war on Gerson. No way were they going to allow Gerson to popularize a natural cure to cancer. He had to leave the "land of the free."

Action Step *Order the wonderful biography of Max Gerson by his grandson, Howard Straus by calling 888.4.GERSON.*

Spiritual and Physical Exercise

Physical exercise has some value, but spiritual exercise is much more important, for it promises a reward in both this life and the next.

—1 Timothy 4:8

Paul is absolutely right. Comparing this brief pilgrimage to the never-ending time frame of eternity, spiritual preparation wins every time. On the other hand, 2,000 years ago, hardly anyone needed physical exercise. To walk ten miles to the next town for a visit was not a problem. Most people were into the intense labor of gardening. Fishing was hard work. Most of the men were skilled stone cutters. I can understand why Paul didn't give high grades to what is popular today—a workout.

Rick Warren in his best seller, *The Purpose Driven Life,* lesson 4, has this insight: "Just as the nine months you spent in your mother's womb were not an end in themselves but preparation for life, so this life is preparation for the next." He then goes on to refer to death as a "birthday" into eternity.

The nine months prepares us for eighty or ninety years on earth and these years are preparation for eternity with the Lord. To me that gives our earthly trek a lot of dignity. Our lifestyle here should be in harmony with all the expectation we dream of in glory.

This morning I praised God as I competed in the Gulf Coast Senior Games, winning gold in the 5 K and 1500 meters racewalk.

That was very physical and I'm tired. But I'm glad. At seventy-six I'm in top physical condition to serve the Lord in whatever ministry He leads me to do. I want to be my best right up to my "birthday."

My daily prayer is that I be fit for whatever He assigns me to.

Action Step *Magnify your spiritual potential with a solid program every day of phusical exercise. Never, however, let your physical routine take priority over your spiritual one. Be sure to get the reward in both this life and the next.*

Yes to Nuts

So their father, Jacob, finally said to them, "If it can't be avoided then at least do this. Fill your bags with the best products of the land. Take them to the man as gifts—balm, honey, spices, myrrh, pistachio nuts, and almonds."

Genesis 43:11

Nuts are still wonderful gifts and are some of the best products of the land. In a recent report, it was revealed that people eating nuts (peanuts, walnuts, almonds) at least five times a week, lived on average seven years longer. Nut eaters also benefitted by experiencing a lower incidence of heart attacks. Yes, nuts are high in fat, but it is the good kind of fat, polyunsaturated and monounsaturated.

In the category of finger foods, nuts are a favorite. To prepare Crispy Almonds, mix four cups of skinless almonds with one tablespoon of sea salt in pure water and leave in a warm place over night. Drain in a colander. Spread on a baking pan and place in a warm oven (no more than 150 degrees) from 12 to 24 hours, stirring occasionally until dry.

Nuts are good for you. Now the FDA has made it official: Eating 1.5 ounces a day (about a handful or 1/3 cup) of certain nuts can reduce your risk of heart disease—provided you also watch the amount of saturated fat and cholesterol you consume. What nuts qualify? Almonds, hazelnuts, pecans, pistachios and walnuts pass the test. There are about thirty almonds in 1.5 ounces.

To get the best nourishment from nuts, they should be raw and soaked overnight before eating. Almond butter is a much healthier alternative to peanut butter. Place two cups of the soaked almonds along with 1 teaspoon of sea salt in a food processor and grind to a fine powder. Add 3/4 cup of coconut oil along with two tablespoons of raw honey and process until it becomes a smooth butter.

Action Step *Follow the example of Jacob—give a new priority to nuts in your daily nutritional intake. Crack the nuts yourself.*

The Blessings of Barley

There is a young boy here with five barley loaves and two fish. But what good is that with this huge crowd?

—John 6:9

We know that barley was an important food item in Bible times.

It's mentioned thirty-six times. Because it is the first grain crop to come up in the spring, a sheaf of barley was to be waved before the Lord as an offering in the Festival of Firstfruits.

The merits of the juices of newly sprouted grains had been known for years. But it took a Japanese medical doctor, Yoshihide Hagiwara with a background in pharmaceutical research to produce evidence that barley grass is one of the richest sources of nutrients in the botanical world.

It took Dr. Hagiwara several years to perfect a laboratory that would extract the juice from the young barley stems and then remove the water at room temperature. What's left is a rich, concentrated, dark green, fluffy powder. The powder is the essence of barley. It is a *super food*, complete with all the live enzymes.

Enzymes are the workers of all the body's systems. Every chemical and physiological process is carried out by the genius of enzymes. Only with a complete set of enzymes can a food be called "live." The dried barley juice also is replete with *chlorophyll*, the "blood" of the plant. It has proven to be a wound healer of bed sores, throat problems and ulcer cases. It also seems to aid in overcoming allergies as well as stem the proliferation of arthritis.

The green barley concentrate, believe it or not, is 40 percent protein by weight. All the essential amino acids are represented. This is truly a complete food. The latest American version of the Japanese discovery is BarleyMax. I take it every day.

Action Step *Everyone needs this daily blessing. Take a teaspoon of BarleyMax three times a day on an empty stomach. Feed your cells this banquet and be happy.*

Doctor, Heal Thyself

Being wise is as good as being rich, in fact, it is better. Wisdom or money can get you almost anything, but it's important to know that only wisdom can save your life.

—Ecclesiastes 7:11,12

Joe Nicholes M.D. was born in 1909. His great-great grandfather had a plantation in South Carolina. That land became exhausted so his great grandfather pioneered in Tennessee. That land played-out so his grandfather sought virgin land in Alabama. When his father saw that the land was becoming depleted, he moved west to new land in Arkansas. This fertile land gave young Joe and the other kids good food while growing up.

Joe finished medicine and began practice in 1932 in the midst of the great depression. In 1936 Dr. Nicholes built a small general hospital in Atlanta, Texas. Ten years later he suffered an almost fatal heart attack. For the whole next year he lived on nitroglycerin pills. One day he read a statement that said that people who eat natural food grown on fertile soil did not have heart disease. At first he paid no attention to this "food faddism." But soon he was struck by the book written by Sir Albert Howard *An Agricultural Testament.*

From that day on Joe's passion became a search for the science behind *fertile soil, and natural food* and how the two are the basis of *true health.* He slowly converted his 1,000 acre ranch into an organic farm. He became president of Natural Food Associates. His advice to his patients was, "Never eat a food that will not spoil, but eat it before it does." Unlike the average M.D. who dies at the age of 58, Joe Nicholes lived to a ripe old age.

Action Step *Learn from history. Do all you can to conserve and build up whatever land you use. Pray that more physicians convert to wholeness.*

Bypassing the Bypass

The hearts of the wise lead them to do right, and the hearts of the foolish lead them to do evil.

—Ecclesiastes 10:2

Gene Smith and I were in the Army Air Force at the same time and at the same base. But we didn't meet until fifty years later at the Bradenton Missionary Village where we both lived. Gene had a serious heart condition—he lived one day at a time. I told him there were options. Once he read what I gave him, he decided he would do two things, change his diet and begin *chelation* (key-lay-shon).

Even though no one expected him to live more than a year, Gene lived seven more healthier years before saying goodbye.

Without the dangers, risks and pain of drugs and surgery, there is a safe, easy way of defusing the *ticking time bomb* of arteries filled with plaque. Chelation is a way of cleaning them out. It pulls the calcium out of one's arteries and puts it back in the bones where you need it. How is it done?

The bottle of therapy solution is dripped into the vein over a period of about four hours. The main therapeutic agent is EDTA (ethylene diamine tetra-acetic acid). It has a special affinity to metals. It attaches itself to them and drags them out into the circulation where it is later excreted with the wastes.

Over 500,000 people have benefitted from chelation. Yet it's surprisingly unknown outside natural health circles. Is that because angioplasty and bypass surgery are a $16 billion-a-year business for doctors and hospitals?

Chelation has also become an important adjunct in the treatment of environmental problems such as allergies, asthma and chronic fatigue syndrome. Vision, hearing and memory have also improved.

Action Step *Get the facts about chelation. Talk to someone who has experienced chelation. Make up your own mind. A non-invasive, non-toxic remedy makes sense.*

Laugh Your Way to Health

A cheerful heart is good medicine, but a broken spirit saps a person's strength.

—Proverbs 17:22

Fighting illness has never been so much fun. I'm talking about using humor and laughter. Stress just melts away while laughing through a funny video. The person that best called our attention to this was Norman Cousins. In his book he tells the story of how he cured himself of a terminal disease, ankylosing spondylitis.

His pain was so severe that even morphine would not help. When he realized he was dying, he checked himself out of the hospital and moved into a hotel room. He rented all the old comedy movies he could get his hands on. He first discovered that ten minutes of belly laughter would give him enough relief to sleep for two hours. He continued viewing these humorous films, laughing himself to sleep. His pain became less and less a problem and he began to feel stronger and stronger. He went on to a complete cure and lived twenty more years pain free.

After Cousin's book revealed this remarkable therapy of laughter, researchers started to find reasons for his getting well. What they found was that laughter greatly activated the immune system. There is a decrease in the neuroendocrine hormones that come with stress and a spontaneous increase in the activity of the T cells, B cells and immunoglobulins. Laughter is truly good medicine.

Generally we are far too serious. We need to lighten up, enjoy life more and look for more things to celebrate. Not long ago I ordered a video of Dick Van Dyke in six big episodes in black and white. Talk about enjoying clean comedy and laughing all through it. We sleep so well after some good belly laughter.

> **Action Step** *Work at keeping your heart cheerful. Maybe it'll take an old Popeye video to bring back the sparkle in your eyes. Make God smile as you praise Him continually.*

How We Die

When Jacob had finished giving instructions to his sons, he drew his feet up into the bed, breathed his last and was gathered to his people.

—Genesis 49:33

Could this be a model for the way all saints could bless their family and quietly go to be with the Lord? Jacob died at the age of 147. As he sensed death was at the door, he summoned all his sons to tell them "what is going to happen to you in the days to come" (Genesis 49:1). These predictions and blessings show how mentally alert he was just minutes before his death.

I categorized this Jacob event as just another Bible miracle, until I saw it reenacted before my eyes in 1981 in Colombia. In one of my ministry trips into the vast rural areas, I met Blas Garcia. His daughter was one of the core group to plant the first church in the south/east area of Monteria. Blas suddenly called his daughter and all the other children to come home at the ranch. Blas and his nine children celebrated for a week. Then he gathered his son and eight daughters around him. He blessed each one of them and laid down saying these words, "Be quiet and let me go quietly to my heavenly Father." Within one hour he was dead.

Not long ago a lady who lived in our village, in her mid nineties, sensed that her body was shutting down. First she stopped driving her car. A week later she announced she would no longer ride her bicycle. A week later she stopped coming to the cafeteria and a month later she quietly passed on into the arms of Jesus. No sirens, no hospital, no diagnosis, she slipped into eternity naturally. Isn't this the way God intends for all of us to go?

Action Step *Pray that your demise be a natural one. Plan well in advance how you will gather your loved ones to bless them just before you bid adieu to planet earth. Do what more of us are doing or plan on doing, to die healthy.*

Eat Good Fats and Oils

You must never eat fat or blood. This is a permanent law for you and all your descendants, wherever they may live.

—Leviticus 3:17

When the Bible talks about fat, it is referring to the very evident tallow seen among the entrails and around the kidneys. Our problem today is that, unlike the animals of Bible times whose meat had only 4% fat, our cattle have meat with up to 30% fat. To comply with the above command, we would have to stop eating meat altogether.

Yet fats and oils are essential to life. Actually, many people carried away by the no-fat craze, are lacking these essential lipids in their diet. There are two essential oils (the body needs them but can't make them), omega 3 and omega 6, that we have to get in our diet. The best source is a tablespoon of flax seed oil taken every day.

The real villians are the **trans fats**. These are man-made fats by adding nitrogen to otherwise acceptable oils. They are unnatural, can't be used by the body, get in the way and do harm. We must **avoid** them. Foods that are the highest in trans fats are bread, rolls, crackers, biscuits and doughnuts. When McDonald switched from beef tallow to hydrogenated vegetable oil, the percentage of trans fats in their french fries increased from 5% to 40%. Neal Barnard M.D. was right when he said, "When you see the golden arches you're probably on the road to the pearly gates."

The man I look up to when it comes to fats is Udo Erasmus PhD. His program is called "The Right Fat Diet." If you want to investigate further check out the web site florahealth.com and be convinced that fats and oils are key to vibrant health.

Action Step *Develop the habit of reading labels to look for oil that has been hydrogenized. Rid you diet of as much animal fat as possible. "Butter" your bread with extra virgin olive oil. Make the switch from a frying pan to an electric wok.*

Fearfully and Wonderfully Made

Thank you for making me so wonderfully complex. Your workmanship is marvelous—and how well I know it.

—Psalm 139:14

What better illustration could there be of how the body sustains itself than the miracle of healing. Cuts, bruises and burns are a part of life. Given enough time, almost all body insults will heal. Healing takes place in three phases.

The first phase, inflamation, occurs immediately. Redness, heat and swelling indicate that the ingredients for healing are gathering at that location. White cells engulf and destroy bacteria, fibrogen seals the wound's edges and tissue regeneration begins.

The second phase, proliferation, takes two to three weeks. New blood vessels form and fibroblasts synthesize collagen. The scab forms. Only when the wound is well covered, does the scab slough off. This signals the third and longest stage of healing. The remodeling may take up to two years yielding a softer scar.

Three years ago I decided to read our mail while riding my new bicycle home. I took my hands off of the handlebars. Suddenly one foot slipped off the peddle and to the ground. The handlebar turned 90 degrees and I went flying over the front of the bicycle. My forehead, elbows and knees were a bloody mess.

Being in good shape physically, I got up and peddled home. I immediately washed, thoroughly, the badly damaged areas. Then I took a leaf of an aloe vera plant, pealed it and scraped up a half glass of its wonderful leaf juice. I applied this liberally on all the wounds.

Four hours later I did it again the same way. The following five days I repeated the natural treatment once a day. Within ten days all signs of the accident were gone. No medicines—just God, a body that is wonderfully made and one of God's blessed herbs.

Action Step *Maintain fearfully what God made so wonderfully. Supplement with extra vitamin C and A as well with the proteolytic enzyme bromelain if wounds are extensive.*

Choose Life

Today I have given you the choice between life and death, between blessing and curses. I call on heaven and earth to witness the choice you make. Oh, that you would choose life, that you and your descendants might live.
—Deuteronomy 30:19

We had transferred to the States to work in Mission administration, so Nazario, a Colombian pastor, wrote to me saying, "Last year I had open-heart surgery. At the same time I suffered with an ulcer—for one month I was between life and death. The doctors insist that I stop working and retire near the big city where I can be closely monitored with medication the rest of my life. I have no savings and my five children are still in school. Dr. Piersma, I need your financial assistance."

This is how I answered Nazario: "I will share with you how the Lord guided me to overcome a life-threatening crisis similar to yours. Do what I tell you and you, too, will be restored to complete health. Stop eating white rice. Eat only the natural brown rice. Avoid all dairy products. Sorry, don't drink any more coffee. Eat as much as you can of *raw* spinach, lettuce, carrots and cabbage. Consume papaya and tomatoes every day. Stop all sugar and sweet consumption. Have nothing to do with pork.

Eat one egg a day from the chickens that run loose. Sprout sunflower, alfalfa and mung seeds for your salads. Begin an exercise program and plant a vegetable garden. In two months begin to wean yourself off drugs. In six months you will be a new man. Pray for the miracle of discipline. CHOOSE LIFE!"

A year later I was in Colombia teaching wellness to the pastors when Nazario came up and hugged me. He was totally well and preaching like never before.

Action Step *Choose to prevent a Nazario-like crisis. Learn how closely linked our health is to what we eat. Consume foods more in the form God made them. Think twice if it comes in a box.*

Dietary Fiber

Her hands are busy spinning thread, her fingers twisting fiber.
—Proverbs 31:19

These same beautiful hands can wisely provide fiber for her family in her meal planning. No one preached dietary fiber more than Dr. Denis Burkitt, veteran medical missionary in Africa. He noticed that Africans, where he was, did not suffer the same disease conditions that plagued Americans. One of the most common abdominal surgeries in America is for appendicitis but Burkitt had never seen a case in Africa. Why? They had lots of fiber.

Another complication that can be avoided with dietary fiber is the hiatal hernia. A common symptom is heartburn. What actually happens is this: when the muscles of the abdominal wall contract to assist in the evacuation of a constipated stool, pressure within the abdomen is increased, and as a result, the upper end of the stomach is squeezed up out of the abdomen into the thorax.

Hemorrhoids and varicose veins are two more conditions that will not happen if we get enough fiber in our diet. When the normal anal cushions are forced out by a fiber-depleted diet, it becomes very painful. Varicose veins are not caused by pregnancy. Once again it's the abdominal pressure that triggers the malfunction of the vein valves. These valves prevent backflow but pressure balloons the wall of the veins to the point where the blood flows back, away from the heart.

Why is colon cancer twelve times more prevalent among black Americans than with Africans? Diet, of course. How does fiber protect against colon cancer? One, it increases bulk and thus dilutes carcinogens. Two, it increases the acidity of stools, cutting down bacterial production of carcinogens.

Action Step *Make sure your diet has whole-grain cereals and flour, brown rice, fresh fruit, dried prunes, nuts, flax seed, beans and raw vegetables. For a good colon cleanse to begin with, I recommend the powder, Fiber Cleanse by Hallelujah Acres.*

Where Is Your Courage?

Yet our God gave us the courage to declare his Good News to you
boldly, even though we were surrounded by many who opposed us.
—1 Thessalonians 2:2

The following is a collage of fragments from a speech of the Honorable Berkley Bedell on 12/14/93 to the New York Assembly's Committees on Higher Education and Health: "I left Congress because I contracted Lyme Disease from a tick bite. I was treated three times with conventional treatments. Each day I had a strong antibiotic injected into my vein for six weeks. Each time I would feel a little better and then symptoms would return.

"I then turned to an unconventional treatment. I submitted some Lyme germs to a lab run by veterinarians. They injected these spirochetes into the udder of a pregnant cow. At the birth of the calf they processed the colostrum. I took a tablespoon of this whey every hour. My symptoms disappeared, I clearly no longer have Lyme Disease. This treatment cost $500 as compared to the $26,000 I paid for the drugs that didn't work.

"The same happened with my prostate cancer. The surgical removal of the gland and the subsequent radiation that cost $10,000 didn't work—the cancer came back. In Canada, however, I found how to flood the area with nitrogen. For twenty-one days I gave myself an injection. This cost me $600 and I no longer have cancer.

"Americans are repeatedly told that they are unable to make sound decisions about their own health. But I've found dedicated practitioners who hold great promise. However, they are being stopped at every turn because these new ways are called quackery.

"Are we going to let the international drug firms sustain a monopoly with toxic medicines of limited effectiveness? There is a growing army of angry people demanding a greater say in healthcare. *Mr. Chairman and committee, where is your courage?*"

Action Step *Join ranks with those who are fighting for healthcare freedom. Give your opinions at hearings!*

Are Sin and Sickness Related?

But afterward Jesus found him in the temple and told him, "Now you are well; so stop sinning, or something even worse may happen to you."

—John 5:14

Along side the pool of Bethesda, near the temple, lay many sick people. Jesus directed His words to one of them and asked the paralytic if he would like to get well. He had been immobile for thirty-eight years so his response was anything but positive. Jesus ignored this and commanded him to get up and walk. Instantly, he was healed.

Jesus' follow-up counsel to him was brief. For his total good, physical and spiritual, Jesus told him to stop sinning. This healed paralytic was typical of many Jews of that day. He had turned his back on all the wisdom of God's Word and followed the "excitement" of the Greek games and their pagan views of life. He left the safety of Hebrew law and sanitation by eating and drinking with the heathen. He feasted on pork and strong drink. His sinful lifestyle resulted in his becoming an invalid.

What he needed to do was repent. Pentecost would soon trumpet the full answer to his quest for complete healing; body and soul. Jesus, who saves, told him he should *stop sinning*. He was to remember what he was taught as a child in his new life. This new peace, the secret of *shalom*, was all centered around Jesus the Messiah. Knowing Him was the source of power to change and stop sinning.

Fast forward. I see Jesus saying these same words to many who are ill today. We've been sidetracked from the *Way and Truth and Life* into the way of the world—eating and drinking as they do. No wonder that most of us are less than vigorous due to degenerative conditions. Could our problem be sin? I'm sure it was in my case. *Remember, it is sin to know what you ought to do and then not do it* (James 4:17).

Action Step *STOP doing what you know is unfavorable to your health—it's a sin. Get better instead of worse.*

81

Don't Take Eyesight for Granted

Turn and answer me, O Lord my God! Restore the light to my eyes, or I will die.

—Psalm 13:3

Few things are as devastating as having to spend your golden years unable to see. Before my "eyes" were opened to the biblical secrets of wellness, I helplessly stood by watching my parents go blind or nearly so. Dad's case was macular degeneration and mother's was a botched cataract operation. Neither could read and Dad had to give up driving.

Like most people I considered these things as par with getting older. I had no idea eye diseases could be prevented as well as being reversed once they are discovered. What I found out was that eye problems don't happen because of age—they are the result of damage which occurs over your lifetime and then manifests itself in later years.

As in the case of all other illnesses, nutrition plays a major role.

I am convinced that a lifetime of eating right will keep one's sight in good health right to the end. Experts advise that we eat plenty of carrots and their juice. Add to this the dark, leafy green vegetables as well as tomatoes and brightly colored fruits.

The primary vision problems that people have as they age are cataracts, macular degeneration, glaucoma and retinopathy. Medicine and surgery attempt to slow the pace to eventual blindness. But, thank God, there are other options that are promising. Ophtalmologist E.A. Lucidi says, "I can tell you that most blindness can be prevented or stopped if caught in time. I have seen great success in people taking the right supplements." The right supplements should have in them: Lutein, Lipoic Acid, Lycopene, Bilberry, Gingo Biloba, Zeaxanthin and Eyebright. I'll be taking all of these in the same capsule the rest of my life. The Lord willing, I'll avoid what my parents suffered.

Action Step *Don't forget to exercise and massage your eyes. Go to drwhitaker.com for details concerning the supplement.*

Vaccines: Are They Safe?

Wisdom will multiply your days and add years to your life. If you become wise, you will be the one to benefit. If you scorn wisdom, you will be the one to suffer.

—Proverbs 9:11,12

Case #1: Harold reacted to his DPT shot with 104 degree fever and high-pitched screaming. Harold is blind today. Case #2: Kate was 4 months old when she received the DPT shot. Within 72 hours she was shrieking in pain. Today she continues to have seizures and cannot speak.

Case #3: Stacey received her measles shot at 16 months. On the 10th day her temperature shot up to 107 degrees. She was panting, struggling to breathe and had ongoing seizures. She has never been the same.

In the year 2002 there were 5,309 vaccine-related deaths reported. Hats off to the United Press who did a four-year probe into the big, bad vaccine business. On July 20, 2003 the story broke. It zeroed in on vaccines made by Wyeth that contained a mercury-based preservative thimerosal, suspected of causing autism.

The Polio epidemic of the thirties and forties had already declined 60 percent before the introduction of the vaccine. And there is no scientific evidence that it influenced its disappearance. It actually caused it to increase. It is known that 87 percent of all the polio cases between 1973 and 1983 were *caused* by polio vaccine.

The same happens with measles. At least 58 percent of all cases were contracted by people who were vaccinated against the disease.

There is no federal law requiring any vaccination and all the state laws allow exemptions. It can be a tough battle for parents who choose *not* to have their children vaccinated, but you can win.

Action Step *Be wise. Get the forms to fill out to avoid shots from the National Health Federation. Order the book* Vaccinations, Deception & Tragedy *by Michael Dye of Hallelijah Acres. Thank God for new insights.*

Don't Guess...Muscle Test

Truth stands the test of time; lies are soon exposed.

—Proverbs 12:19

Just as all the authorities five hundred years ago were convinced the world was flat, even so today the average Christian thinks that muscle testing is New Age. Let me assure you that this bio-feedback tool is pure science. Just because modern medicine is stuck in chemistry and germs does not limit the Lord to continually reveal new dimensions to His servants.

Dr. David Frahm, Naturopath (ND), author of best-seller, *A Cancer Battle Plan,* has published a ninety-six-page manual entitled *How to Be Your Own Best Nutritionist*. In this marvelous presentation, Frahm explains how he first saw this tool being used to save the life of his dying wife. Anne was declared terminal due to the return of breast cancer. Muscle Response Testing (MRT) was employed to: 1- identify nutritional deficiencies, 2- identify foods to be avoided, and 3- identify supplements that would help address deficiencies.

The doctor had Anne place her finger on the various acupuncture points on her body and then tested the strength of her shoulder muscle while her arm was outstretched. If the muscle weakened, that indicated a weakness of that particular organ. Where weak points were detected, an herbal product historically known to be helpful would be held to the specific point as the indicator muscle was retested. The previously weak point would become strong. The implication was that the product tested would help strengthen the weakness or deficiency in the body.

With the help of the ND and her "detoxifying-strengthening" regime, Anne won back her health. A bone marrow tap by her oncologist showed no cancer. "It's either your diet or divine intervention," he said. The Frahms knew it was both. MRT is based on the fact that all things have vibrational energy.

Action Step *Stop taking vitamins you may not need—test first. Do what we did; get the manual and start learning how to do it.*

Sweat Your Way to Radiant Health

All your life you will sweat to produce food . . .

—Genesis 3:19

The *sauna* has become a way of life for many Scandinavian people. It is credited for much of the rugged vitality and endurance of the Finnish people. These wet steam rooms produced benefits such as getting rid of body toxins, weight loss and death to viruses.

Today, however, with water being in itself so polluted, most have opted for the safer and more effective *dry sauna*. It is technically called *Far Infrared Sauna Therapy*.

In the phone booth-looking sauna that can seat one to four persons, the special bulbs radiate the infrared rays directly on the person. Radiant heat is simply a form of energy that heats objects directly through a process called conversion, without having to heat the air in between. The infrared heat in this health system is just like the heat from our sun. This sauna may induce two or three times the sweat volume than a hot-air sauna does, while operating at a cooler air range.

As you can see, the sauna brings about perfuse sweating. It is sweating that translates into vibrant health. True, a marathon runner will get in shape sooner, but how many of us can run twenty to thirty miles a week? Sitting in a sauna closet is a way to give the heart a good workout without running. Sweating 500 grams is the equivalent to running 3 miles. Due to the deep penetration of the rays into the skin, the deep-heating effect produces a sought-after cardiovascular conditioning as the body works to cool itself.

The infrared thermal system can play a pivotal role in weight control. In a thirty minute session one can burn a thousand calories.

For those who have touches of arthritis, bursitis or any muscle pain, the dry sauna can't be beat. Any condition associated with poor circulation would be greatly benefitted.

Action Step *Visit a spa to see the sauna and imagine where it would fit in your home. Don't fear a little fever, it cures anything.*

End Your Addiction

You may say, "I am allowed to do anything." But I reply, "Not everything is good for you." And even though "I am allowed to do anything," I must not become a slave to anything.

—1 Corinthians 6:12

Here Paul is spelling out God's ordinance against any addiction.

Being *a slave to anything* is not acceptable. Victoria Boutenko is one of America's foremost nutrition teachers. Her passion is to help all of us overcome our addiction to COOKED FOOD.

Fifteen years ago she, her husband, Igor, and children, Sergei and Valya, (they came from Russia) were all chronically ill. None of the remedies worked. But everything changed for good when they switched—cold turkey, to an ALL RAW DIET. They've had super health ever since.

An addiction to cooked food starts at six months of age when mother forces the baby to eat it. Since it is harder to change from cooked foods than for alcoholics to get sober, Victoria launched "Rawfooders Anonymous" and wrote the book *12 Steps to Raw Foods*. Victoria teaches that the whole transition process is motivated by an intense spiritual focus. Since hanging on to one percent cooked food will keep us craving, her Step 1 says it is important we admit we have a cooked food dependency.

In Step 2 one declares that live vegan food is the most natural diet for a human being. Step 3 teaches the necessary skills and recipes in preparing live food. In Step 4 we learn to live in harmony with people who eat cooked food. Step 5 shows how to avoid temptation. Step 6 creates support groups. Step 7 finds alternative activities to eating. Step 8, personality repatterning, Step 9 points out the psychology of food addiction, Step 10 is trusting one's intuition, Step 11 and 12 show the joy and growth of the movement.

Action Step *Start with some minor addictions before tackling the big one. Go to rawfamily.com and order the books.*

Strength for Today and Everyday

May the bolts of your gates be of iron and bronze; may your strength match the length of your days.

—Deuteronomy 33:25

These words are a part of the blessing Moses gives to the tribe of Asher, as he did with all the tribes just before he died at the age of 120. The account of his death in the next chapter says that he was *as strong as ever*. Strong, at the age of 120? Could this mean that Moses died healthy?

A half century ago Dr. Paul Bragg ND, Ph.D. died at the age of ninety-seven of a surfboard accident. As a teenager, Bragg was dying of tuberculosis. He chose LIFE, however, doing what scripture exhorted him to do. He became an example of how to get well and stay well. God used him to teach thousands of people how to stay strong to the very end.

Aging is usually associated with such things as gray hair, balding, wrinkles and loss of physical strength. And this is what we see in most cases. Our verse today, however, insinuates that our strength, our vigor, our zest for life, can be a daily experience until the day we leave our temples to be with Him forever.

I believe this biblical example of Moses as well as the case of Bragg, challenge us who are living in the last days to be *as strong as ever*. What excuse do we have to *not* be strong spiritually and strong physically throughout *the length of our days*. These men give us the vision to be able to pass on to glory in a state of vigor, wholeness and with a sound mind.

It is true that we have an allotted time on this planet earth. But that is why we need to take advantage of each *numbered* day we have. It's never too late to start putting in practice the lifestyle changes that will empower our whole being.

Action Step *Work out a program that will transform your life, even without the games that predispose you to being strong. Be a person Jesus would be proud of. Give God the glory.*

Tooth Decay Is Not Necessary

Your teeth are as white as newly washed sheep. They are perfectly matched; not one is missing.

—Song of Songs 6:6

In the early 1930s, a Cleveland dentist named Weston Price traveled to isolated parts of the globe to discover factors responsible for good dental health. Among the peoples who were still isolated enough to have traditional diets, he discovered they had beautiful, straight teeth with freedom from decay. They also had fine physiques and were healthy.

The isolated groups Dr. Price investigated understood the importance of preconceptual nutrition for both parents. Long-life dental health starts at conception and is developed during gestation. Babies born from healthy parents will never need braces when they are teenagers. A healthy rounded face will handsomely provide plenty room for dental arches for the well spaced thirty-two teeth. These teeth should last a lifetime.

"People often go through many doctors and therapies in search of answers for their problems, never realizing that their chronic conditions may be traceable to dental complications," states Gary Verigan DDS. The first complication is the mercury amalgam. These silver fillings are implicated in Alzheimer's, mental illness, MS and cancer. Another questionable dental fix is the root canal. In a few cases, toxins have built up and poisoned the whole body.

The habit of brushing your teeth is a good one. But you may want to brush with something other than toothpaste because the glycerine in pastes blocks the re-enamelization process. Use bar soap or better yet, use a special Hand Soap, an advanced hygiene system in a tub. Our annual dental bill is only a fraction of what it was when we were using the usual toothpastes.

A postscript from Dr. Price's observations in Zimbabwe: "By 1980 western foods such as white bread, sugar, jam and tea had become popular and with it came diabetes, high blood pressure and dental caries."

Action Step *Attention prospective parents: The future of your baby's smile depends on your health at the time of conception. eat nutrient dense whole foods. Avoid silver amalgams. Brush your teeth with soap instead of paste.*

Pray for the Sick

Are any among you sick? They should call for the elders of the church and have them pray over them, anointing them with oil in the name of the Lord. And their prayer offered in faith will heal the sick, and the Lord will make them well. And anyone who has committed sins will be forgiven. Confess your sins to each other and pray for each other so that you may be healed.

—James 5:14–16

When we pray for the sick, it is wise to follow the counsel in verse 16 first. The elders need to encourage the ill person to confess. Yes, to confess everything he perceives as sin in his life. The elders should ask him why he thinks he is sick because disease always has a cause. Most people bring sickness upon themselves by self-indulgence, eating like the world does.

The ill person needs to confess his sins of unhealthy practices and perverted appetite. The elders can then feel free to follow the protocol of verse 14.

Praying for the sick is a very solemn exercise and should not be done without careful consideration. In many cases of prayer for the healing of the sick, that which is called faith is nothing less than presumption. If these persons gain the blessing of health, many would continue the same lifestyle of fast food and bad habits. Their reasoning is that if God heals them in answer to prayer they are at liberty to continue their unhealthy habits and indulge without restraint. If God would miraculously heal these persons, He would be encouraging sin.

However, if the patient confesses his faults and receives the wise counsel of the elders regarding healthy habits, the Lord can heal and not encourage further sin. Rarely is it God's will that we become ill, but we do get sick. Too often, however, our first reaction is to shrug our shoulders and say, "It must be God's will."

Actually, it's a disregard for God's natural laws.

Action Step *Do it in the right order: confession, acceptance of the elder's advice, anoint with oil and pray for healing.*

Soils Determine Health

Plant and harvest your crops for six years, but let the land rest and lie fallow during the seventh year.

—Exodus 23:10–11

As our soils go, so goes our nutrition and our health, so writes Tom Valentine in *Search for Health*, vol. 2 #4, 1994. Tom suggests that we compare the taste between the typical supermarket tomato and the ones Dad and Mother grow in their vegetable garden. The contrast is due to the mineral content, so delicious in the home-grown tomato. The commercial tomato is grown on chemical laden fields. Dad's are organically grown using compost.

Everyone must eat to live. Agriculture and food production are the nation's largest business. To live well we have to eat well. On top of the fact that the harvest is nutritionally deficient as it comes from the farms, the food becomes doubly deficient when it is refined and processed to provide "shelf life." Our nation's food supply is woefully inadequate.

Much after the example of the Israelites, my grandfather rotated his crops, used only natural manures for fertilizer and allowed plots to *lie fallow* every four or five years. No wonder my mother was so vigorous and healthy her whole life. She was raised on a farm that followed the biblical principle.

Chemical salt fertilizers have contributed greatly to depleted soils. They lack necessary minerals and trace elements. The soils are also depleted of balanced bacterial life—and just like our own digestive tracts, a balanced flora is required for optimal soil health.

And because the earth worms no longer find the cropland hospitable, the soil becomes compacted and no longer holds the moisture. It becomes like a duck's back.

Our options are: grow our own vegetables, get them directly from an organic farm or buy them at a health store.

Action Step *Become a partner in an organic farm. Cover all the nutritional bases by taking a complete multivitamin/mineral.*

A Gift for Ministry

Are you called to help others? Do it with all the strength and energy that God supplies. Then God will be given glory in everything through Jesus Christ.
—1 Peter 4:11

Helping others is a lifelong purpose of every believer. The Lord has given us bodies that are strong enough to carry out what we need to do. One of the most important glands of our body that orchestrates the supply of energy is the *thyroid.*

The thyroid gland lies in the neck, just below the Adam's apple.

It measures about two inches across and normally can't be seen. The thyroid secrets hormones which control the body's metabolic rate. When the gland is producing too little hormone, lack of energy is one of the first symptoms to appear.

Dr. David Frahm of Health*Quarters* warns us that thyroid deficiency is very often a major player in many diseases. Not only do we see dry skin, weight loss, sluggishness and infertility but hypothyroid contributes to the onset of heart disease and cancer.

Low thyroid should be confirmed by the Barnes temperature test. Do it by taking the armpit temperature the first thing in the morning. If the reading is under 97.8, low thyroid function can be suspected. Frahm points out that low thyroid is a *nutritional* problem to be treated with a supplement.

The basic problem is the lack of dietary iodine. The best source of iodine is seaweed. Oriental peoples eat sea vegetables and rarely have thyroid problems. One of the best sources of organic iodine is kelp.

Action Step *Worship God with zeal. Since we do not get enough iodine from the salt, take the precaution of taking a daily supplement. Four drops of Jensen's LIQUI-DULSE in water each day is all you'll need.*

Pride and Prejudice

All those who touch a dead body and do not purify themselves in the proper way defile the Lord's Tabernacle and will be cut off from the community of Israel.

—Numbers 19:13

Over 3,500 years ago God gave definite instructions concerning sanitation, health and diet but man has consistently ignored them.

Take for instance the case of Ignaz Semmelweis, a Hungarian doctor around 1850.

He noticed that a deadly contagion was being transmitted into his hospital ward. One of every six women in the OB ward were dying. Semmelweis suspected that this disaster was due to the lack of hand washing on the part of the examining doctors. He noticed that they would go from performing autopsies directly into doing vaginal exams with unwashed hands.

Semmelweis ordered doctors to wash their hands before doing diagnostic exams. The death rates dropped to one in every eighty-four maternal cases. Were they convinced? On the contrary, lazy students, prejudiced obstetricians and jealous superiors scorned and belittled Ignaz, so much that his annual contract was not renewed.

His successor threw out the wash basins and up shot the mortality rate to where it was before. This so affected Dr. Semmelweis that he was committed to an insane asylum. He died at the age of forty-two, possibly from the beatings of asylum guards.

How can this possibly be? you are thinking. This whole scenario happened only a 150 years ago. We were well into the scientific epoch by then. How can evident proof be ignored? Well, hasn't the same thing happened recently with the cigarette hearings? Thousands of us go on smoking, completely ignoring the alarming lung cancer statistics. How many forward-thinking individuals like Dr. Semmelweis do we have today, being blocked by prejudice?

Action Step *Be a visionary in the world of your expertise. Are you willing to be "crucified" so that mankind be set free?*

Total Health: A Christian World View

Dear friend, I am praying that all is well with you and that your body is as healthy as I know your soul is.

—3 John 2

How healthy is your soul? If your soul is well, then your body should be equally well. Why? Because through God's initiative we have *total health and well-being.*

In Galatians 1:3–4 there is basis for *freedom from sin.*
In Philippians 4:8–9 there is basis for *freedom from distress.*
In Psalm 103:3 there is basis for *freedom from illness.*

Man's response to God's initiative is
worship
with faith, confession and obedience.

Truly, *salvation* is one big package of *wholeness.* According to Philippians 2:12, this salvation must be continuously worked out. As long as we are alive the Lord expects us to work at staying well—spiritually and physically. We are to be wise stewards with our souls and bodies.

Becoming healthy and staying healthy today requires *work.*

Cooperating with our three billion cells is a challenge. We have to take measures that our great-grandparents didn't have to think about. But today the following are bottomline issues:

Water - We must drink seven to nine glasses of pure water each day.

Cleansing - Have an intestinal program of probiotics and juicing.

Exercise - Do stretching, weight lifting and aerobics.

Living food - Eat freshly harvested organic fruits and vegetables.

Supplements - Take multivitamins, minerals and antioxidants.

Action Step *Claim total wellness on the authority of God's Word. Experience all that salvation includes. Take steps to work out a daily regimen that brings joy and glory to God.*

Salad Savvy

To those who are open to my teaching, more understanding will be given.
—Luke 8:18

Are you receiving these 101 healthy ways with an open mind? Are you beginning to understand more each time? Today I'll share with you how Donna and I dress our salads. To us, salads have moved from the edge to the center. Instead of being a minor dish to pick at during the meal, it has taken center stage—an entree.

Weekly we go to the local organic vegetable farm and happily select the freshly harvested lettuces. The heads of Romaine are so robust and dark green. Then we chose from the Red Leaf, Boston, Bibb and spinach. At home we remove the bottom attachment, separate the leaves, wash them, spin them to remove the water, situate them into the crisper and put them in the refrigerator.

Half of our salad is lettuce and half is vegetables. There are so many to choose from. The most popular in our home are: carrots, broccoli, cucumber, bell peppers, tomatoes, cilantro, green onions, celery, kale and dandelion. These, all raw and organic, are put in layers throughout the lettuces. One of our favorite and most simple-to-prepare dressings is called the Oil and Vinegar Dressing.

This is the recipe: 3 parts grape seed oil
2 parts raw apple cider vinegar
1–2 parts raw honey

If you are not ready to prepare the dressings from scratch, get the salad dressing mix packs at the local supermarket. Directions on the packet are easy to follow. The important part is to use the right vinegar and oil. For vinegar use apple cider or balsamic. The healthy oils are virgin olive, grape seed or Udo's Choice. Shake the ingredients together in a cruet with a tight-fitting lid.

The last word on salad dressing preparation is in the book *Salad Dressing for Life* by Rhonda Malkmus.

Action Step *Understand that salads are basic to a healthy diet. Pray your taste buds get educated to appreciate raw veggies.*

How to Get Well

If you want to, you can make me well again.

—Matthew 8:2

How to Get Well is the title of a book written by Paavo Airola Ph.D., ND and published in 1974. My copy was one of the 24th printing. I guess many other people before me were impressed with such a title. Who in their right mind would be so bold, so different, so daring and so presumptuous as to think that he has the answers to what the whole world has been asking since Adam and Eve?

Truly, the late Dr. Airola was a great man.

He called his book a handbook for natural healing. He studied biochemistry and biological medicine in Europe. This gave him a good start in a holistic practice. I was excited to get into the book when I read who he was dedicating it to; ". . . to the multitude who suffer and die needlessly, uninformed and unaware that simple, safe and effective means of correcting their ills and restoring health are available . . ." Doesn't that resonate with you?

His opening salvo gets his readers scrambling to put on their seatbelts. Imagine hearing: "In spite of all *our great medical progress,* when in the enlightened future, the true medical history will be written, the 20th century will be known as *the dark ages of the healing art.* Today's concept of disease is not much different from the primitive voodoo concept. The only difference is the 'evil spirits' have been replaced with 'evil germs.' The job of the modern medicine-man is to kill or drive out the evil germs using his magic drugs, thus saving the innocent victim." Are you still there?

How about his basic cause of disease? Airola says that most diseases have the same basic underlying causes. They are the systemic derangement and metabolic disorder brought about by prolonged physical and mental stresses. It actually boils down to a deficiency of minerals.

Action Step *Thank God for professionals that have dared to be different. Help make the 21st century known for total wellness.*

The Doping of Children

Right away a woman came to him whose little girl was possessed by an evil spirit. She had heard about Jesus, and now she came and fell at his feet.

—Mark 7:25

Today our little boys and girls are *possessed* by an evil spirit less easily defined. One of every five of our kids suffer from behavioral problems. They are called attention-deficit disorder (ADD), attention-deficit hyperactivity disorder (ADHD), obsessive-compulsive disorder, etc. The ever-creative drug companies have "come to the rescue" with antidepressants and mood elevators. Doctors are prescribing some ten different toxic drugs for our children and medicating their minds.

Maureen Salaman of *Health Freedom News* reminds us that there are reasons for these perplexing behaviors. She says we are maiming, sickening and addicting our own children in an industrial orgy of chemically altered foods and drugs on a scale so vast as to call into question our collective sanity. Between vending machines, convenience-food school lunches and the overprocessed food of the supermarket, kids experience nutritional deficiencies big time.

Autism has increased 1,000 percent in the U.S. over the course of the past twenty years. A study in Florida points a guilty finger at dairy products. In the milk of cows there is an addictive opiate called casomorphine. It is concentrated in cheese. Eighty percent of the milk is casein and this breaks down in the stomach to produce a peptide, casomorphine, an opiate. Children are eating three times more cheese than they did twenty years ago, resulting in ten times the number diagnosed with autism.

Action Step *Stop drugging the children and begin to feed them the good stuff their bodies crave. Phase out processed and non-foods from their diet.*

Man's Misery Disease

I, too, have been assigned months of futility, long and weary nights of misery.
—Job 7:3

I couldn't believe it, at age fifty five, this sudden onset of dribbling.

What was going on? I had heard enough about prostate troubles to guess what was happening to me. Evidently this gland that is wrapped around the urethra, enlarges and squeezes the urinal tract to the point where it actually begins to limit the normal flow.

R.B. Cherry M.D. of Reginald B. Cherry Ministries, Houston, TX tells us in his monthly letter that there will be 240,000 new cases and 40,000 deaths in 2004 caused by prostate problems. He calls the whole picture an EPIDEMIC. Actually, every man will get it if he lives long enough.

The gradual enlargement of the prostate is called benign prostatic hypertrophy. This is caused by the decreased level of testosterone and the increased level of estrogen that provokes the formation of a potent form of testosterone called dihydrotestosterone. It's this substance that stimulates the growth of the gland.

As you can tell by the statistics, only one-sixth of the cases turn into cancer. Even less would do so if we assisted the body more to control the enlargement with herbs. To deactivate the effect of the dihydro form of testosterone, certain natural substances have proven to be effective. One can tell how effective the supplement is by the number of times one has to get up to urinate during the night. I knew I had to find something better when I was getting up three times a night.

The best prostate supplement, today, will have most of these ingredients: Saw Palmetto, Pygeum, Stinging Nettle Root and Beta Sitosterol. They all come in one capsule.

Action Step *Avoid the misery by controlling the enlargement. Not all Saw Palmetto is created equal—get quality. For more details check out daily-mfg.com.*

I Have a Dream

In the last days, God said, I will pour out my Spirit upon all people. Your sons and daughters will prophesy, your young men will see visions, and your old men will dream dreams.

—Acts 2:17

Many of us remember the historical setting of the human rights movement when Martin Luther King articulated the unforgettable words "I have a dream." If he had not been assassinated, he could now assess and measure how much of his dream has come true. Do you have a dream? I do.

Dreams are not created in a vacuum. God gives us dreams when we are immersed in an episode. Donna and I have close to twenty years of experience in assisted living and nursing homes. Our mission has always been a spiritual one. We lead Bible studies and conduct church services.

The people become very dear to us right up to the time when death separates us. What bothers us is the way most of them spend their last years ill and in wheelchairs. How many times we have addressed our heavenly Father saying, "Does it have to be this way? Why can't the abundant life be a physical blessing that also lasts the entire lifetime? Why can't we die healthy?"

Since I am an old man, I qualify to dream dreams. This is my dream: a retirement community that believes, practices and experiences wellness *till death do us part*. This is not happening today, but I think it could. We have enough information to make it happen. I can visualize it. By faith I can see hundreds of golden-agers free from drugs and free from illnesses.

I truly believe that it is God's will that we be *whole*, spiritually and physically our entire life. Death brought on by disease is not normal. Our bodies are programmed to stay well. I dream about the day when all the saints simply and joyfully die of old age.

Action Step *Get the vision of being normal, healthy and well. Get your church to sponsor a special village of healthy people.*

Do We Have Healthcare Freedom?

You are truly my disciples if you keep obeying my teachings. And you will know the truth, and the truth will set you free.

—John 8:31–32

The U.S. is one of the most free countries in the world. The teachings of Jesus gave our founding fathers the wisdom to write a Constitution that guaranteed freedom. They should have listened, however, to this advice: "Unless we put medical freedom into the Constitution, the time will come when medicine will organize into an undercover dictatorship . . . To restrict the art of healing to one class of men and deny equal privileges to others . . . The Constitution of the Republic should make special provision for medical freedom as well as religious freedom." (Dr. Benjamin Rush, Surgeon-General of George Washington's armies and signer of the Declaration of Independence 1787)

What Dr. Rush warned us about, has happened just like he predicted. There was an equal number of homeopathic, naturopathic and allopathic physicians 150 years ago. In 1849 the allopathic doctors organized the American Medical Association.

They systematically waged a propaganda war to eliminate competition. By 1910 their war on "quackery" was so successful that the AMA has dominated all aspects of medicine ever since. They have convinced the federal, state and local governments that the people must be "protected" from "unproved" products and the practitioners who are not M.D.s

The art of healing is now tightly controlled by *one class of men.*

In the U.S. we *do not have medical freedom.* At the forefront of the battle to win back our medical liberty is the *National Health Federation.* During no other time in history has there been so much bureaucracy to block the exercise of alternative medicine.

Action Step *Join the National Health Federation and order the book Assault on Medical Freedom by P. Joseph Lisa. Pray the truth will set us free. Wisely use the little freedom we do have.*

What More Could I Ask For?

Jesus looked at them intently and said, "Humanly speaking, it is impossible. But not with God. Everything is possible with God."

—Mark 10:27

The Hallelujah Diet and lifestyle consistently give these results:

1. **Longevity** - Vital, active years will be added to your expected lifespan. This is not just extending life, rather it delays the onset of aging and increases the number of vibrant, disease-free years that you can expect to enjoy.

2. **Reversal** - If a disease condition has not gone beyond the point of no return, all kinds of pathology, most illnesses, can be reversed. Aside from accidents, when these factors are adjusted, the body unswervingly gravitates back to its designed state of health; a miracle of God in slow motion. Encouragingly, regardless of how badly health is compromised, the body never forgets how to heal itself. In fact, God and the body are the only two healing agents in existence.

3. **Prevention** - You will no longer suffer the degenerative diseases that are killing us prematurely—diseases such as heart disease, cancer, diabetes, osteoporosis and Alzheimer's.

   If you pay attention to these laws . . . The Lord will keep you free from every disease. Deuteronomy 7:12,15

4. **Wellness** - We are talking about *wholeness*. Once we give our bodies time to detoxify and repair, we can expect to live the rest of our life free of illness, in a state of optimal health. Since we are programmed to die at least by the age of 120, to the very end we should experience full use of our minds, eyes and hearing.

Action Step *Believe that everything is possible. Accept the promise that God will keep you free from every disease.*

The Hallelujah Diet

Don't copy the behavior and customs of this world, but let God transform you into a new person by changing the way you think. Then you will know what God wants you to do, and you will know how good and pleasing and perfect his will really is.

—Romans 12:2

My number one recommendation to everyone, no matter what conditions we are talking about, is the Hallelujah Diet. Because this diet says No to the "sad" standard American diet and Yes to God's first dietary recommendation in the garden of Eden. This is a way to eliminate sickness, to lose weight, to increase energy and to feel great, restore hope and have abundant life.

Breakfast: Upon rising, one teaspoon of BarleyMax powder, either dry, by letting it dissolve in your mouth, or in a couple ounces of distilled water at room temperature, but never in fruit juice.

Mid-Morning: An eight ounce glass of carrot juice. If juice is not available, a piece of juicy fruit or a drink of CarrotMax powder is second best.

Lunch: Just thirty minutes before, a second teaspoon of BarleyMax. Then a raw salad.

Mid-Afternoon: An eight ounce glass of carrot juice. If juice is not available, some carrot or celery sticks are second best.

Supper: Before dinner, another teaspoon of BarleyMax. A large green salad along with a variety of vegetables. After the salad comes the only cooked food of the day—the 15 percent portion of the day's total intake. This could be a baked potato, brown rice, steamed veggies or a whole grain pasta.

Action Step *Be transformed totally. Do the diet cold turkey. At least, start in that direction. Get the book* Don't Have to be Sick.

Appendix

Education materials and products I recommend:

BOOKS

God's Way to Ultimate Health	George H. Malkmus	
Why Christians Get Sick	George H. Malkmus	
Stop the Medicine	Cynthia Foster	
Salad Dressings for Life	Rhonda J. Malkmus	
(Hallelujah Acres 800.915.9355)		
No Need for Speed	John Bingham Rodale	Inc. 2002
One Answer to Cancer	William Kelly	888.477.3618
How to Be Your Own Best Nutritionist	David Frahm	
Healthy Habits David Frahm	Health*Quarters*	719.593.8694
BRAINRECOVERY.COM	David Perlmutter	800.227.2627
Trace Your Genes to Health	Chris Reading	619.462.7600
Today's Technology in Bible Prophesy	Charles Miller	
	(Send $10 check payable to TIP,	
	P.O. Box 21113 Lansing, MI 48909)	

NEWSLETTERS

Search for Health	Call Carotec at 800.522.4279	
Back to the Garden	It's free. Hallelujah Acres	
Health*Quarters Monthly*	719.593.8694 healthquarters.org	
Health & Healing	Julian Whitaker	800.705.5559
Health Freedom News	National Health Fed.	626.357.2182

Genesis Living Food Snacks	217.368.2290 code DP02H-111
BarleyMax and CarrotMax call	Hallelujah Acres, give pin AJD
LIQUI-DULCE	Order from Health*Quarters*
Get Healthy-Stay Balanced	
18 hour course,	Hallelujah Acres
Latin America Mission	*info@lam.org*

(contact the author at piersmanr@juno.com)

To order additional copies of

Nourishing Body and Soul

Have your credit card ready and call:

1-877-421-READ (7323)

or please visit our web site at
www.pleasantword.com

Also available at:
www.amazon.com
and
www.barnesandnoble.com

Printed in the United States
115852LV00006B/76-81/A